Points of Disruption in the Music Education Curriculum, Volume 1

For decades, scholars in the field of music education have recognized the need for growth and change in our approach to teaching music, yet despite these calls for change, the music education curriculum today remains remarkably similar to that of a century ago. *Points of Disruption in the Music Education Curriculum, Volume 1: Systemic Changes* is one of two volumes that bring together applied suggestions, analyses, and best practices for disrupting cycles of replication in the curriculum of K-12 and collegiate music education programs in the United States and beyond, considering disruption as a force for positive change. Identifying specific strategies for interrupting or reimagining traditional practices, the contributors provide music teachers and music educators with a variety of potential practical approaches to creating changes that foster a better musical education at all levels of the curriculum.

This first volume focuses on systemic changes, including topics like professional development, hiring practices, ableism and universal design, rhizomatic learning, and how to implement disruption across the music education profession. Each chapter outlines how readers can take action to implement novel curricular approaches in their own practice. Bringing together five thought-provoking chapters, this concise volume offers a diverse set of concrete strategies that will be useful to a wide range of music education stakeholders, including teachers, administrators, and curriculum designers.

Marshall Haning is Associate Professor and Area Head for Music Education at the University of Florida.

Jocelyn A. Stevens is Associate Professor of Music Education at Truman State University.

Brian N. Weidner is Associate Professor of Music Education at Butler University.

CMS Pedagogies & Innovations in Music
Series Editor: Eric Hung, Music of Asian America Research Center

The *CMS Pedagogies & Innovations in Music* series consists of short studies and manuals from a variety of music disciplines engaged in pedagogical discovery and innovative approaches to learning, creativity, performance, and scholarship. Serving faculty, administrators, instructors, and future instructors, these short-form books provide new ideas and theories about music curricula in higher education; evidence-based discussions on pedagogical methods and emerging methodologies for teaching music; strategies for improving musical careers; and resources for areas of study outside the traditional Western musical canon.

Commercial and Popular Music in Higher Education
Expanding Notions of Musicianship and Pedagogy in Contemporary Education
Edited by Jonathan R. Kladder

Points of Disruption in the Music Education Curriculum, Volume 1
Systemic Changes
Edited by Marshall Haning, Jocelyn A. Stevens, and Brian N. Weidner

Points of Disruption in the Music Education Curriculum, Volume 2
Individual Changes
Edited by Marshall Haning, Jocelyn A. Stevens, and Brian N. Weidner

For more information, please visit: www.routledge.com/CMS-Pedagogies-&-Innovations-in-Music/book-series/CMSPED

Points of Disruption in the Music Education Curriculum, Volume 1

Systemic Changes

Edited by Marshall Haning, Jocelyn A. Stevens, and Brian N. Weidner

NEW YORK AND LONDON

First published 2024
by Routledge
605 Third Avenue, New York, NY 10158

and by Routledge
4 Park Square, Milton Park, Abingdon, Oxon, OX14 4RN

Routledge is an imprint of the Taylor & Francis Group, an informa business

ISBN: 978-1-032-51547-2 (hbk)
ISBN: 978-1-032-53163-2 (pbk)
ISBN: 978-1-003-41064-5 (ebk)

DOI: 10.4324/9781003410645

Typeset in Times New Roman
by Newgen Publishing UK

Contents

Contributors

Lisa Crawford, DMA, is Adjunct Professor for California State University, Northridge, and teaches composition, arranging, and music theory for Los Angeles County High School. She holds a BMus in composition from University of Oregon, two master's degrees in music education and curriculum and instruction from University of the Pacific and holds a DMA in Music Education from University of Southern California. She serves as Chair of the NAfME Composition Council, as President of College Music Society's Southwest Chapter, and has founded the International Alliance for Young Composers and Songwriters. Her research focuses toward creating and composing music with young students, has co-authored and authored book chapters and articles, has published in the *Oxford Handbook of Music Composition Pedagogy*, and presents nationally and internationally for music education conferences.

Christine D'Alexander, DMA, is Associate Professor of music education at Northern Illinois University. She holds degrees in viola performance from Arizona State University (BM) and music education from the University of Southern California (MM, DMA). D'Alexander has been an active music educator both in Illinois and in California, establishing and directing multiple orchestral programs for youth. Her research focuses on children's participation in community youth orchestras and the integration of music programs within under-resourced communities and has been presented in multiple platforms throughout North America, South America, Europe, and Asia. She serves as a Co-Chair and

Commissioner for the International Society for Music Education (ISME) Community Music Activity (CMA).

Amanda R. Draper is an Assistant Professor of music education at Indiana University's Jacobs School of Music and the Director of The MusiColAbility Project, a community outreach program that fosters collaborative music learning and creative music making between Indiana University students and individuals with disabilities in the Bloomington community. Draper was the 2022–2023 Gretsch Fellow in Children's Music with the Fred Rogers Institute. Her academic interests include investigating musical experiences for diverse learners with a focus on music and autism research, disability studies in music, and teacher preparation for special music education. Draper has presented regionally, nationally, and internationally and has articles published in the *Journal of Research in Music Education, Bulletin of the Council for Research in Music Education*, and *Music Educators Journal*.

Marshall Haning is Associate Professor of music education at the University of Florida. He serves in a variety of national and international leadership roles in music education, including Chair of the International Symposia on Assessment in Music Education. Haning's research interests include music education and music teacher education curricula, informal and nonformal approaches to music education, nonperformance music courses, and assessment in music education. He is well-published in scholarly journals and is a frequent presenter at state, national, and international music education conferences. Haning is also in demand as a choral clinician and adjudicator, and has served in this capacity across the United States as well as in Africa, Australia, Europe, and South America.

Tina Huynh is an Assistant Professor of music education at the University of Puget Sound in Tacoma, where she teaches courses in music, education, and music education, and supervises student teachers. Her research interests center around music in childhood, cultural diversity, culturally responsive teaching, and refugees and music making. Her other written works can be found in a variety of peer-reviewed journals and books. She is the creator of the documentary *Songs of Little Saigon* (2021), producer of the documentary *The Resting Place* (2022), and author of *The Vietnamese Children's Songbook* (2023).

Daniel C. Johnson is Professor of music education at the University of North Carolina Wilmington, where he coordinates undergraduate and graduate music education programs. An international authority on Orff-Schulwerk and a Fulbright Scholar, Johnson's scholarship focuses on classroom music instruction, cross-cultural studies, and music listening. A champion of interdisciplinary scholarship, Johnson's research interests also include teachers' professional development and music education in rural schools. He is the editor of *Music Education in Rural America: Policies and Perspectives* (forthcoming). Other publications include his most recent book, *Holistic Musical Thinking* (2024), and *Musical Explorations: Fundamentals Through Experience*, 7th edition (2021).

Elizabeth S. Palmer, DMA, is an Adjunct Professor at the University of Maryland, Baltimore County, in the Department of Music. Previously she was an instrumental music teacher in Prince George's County, Maryland, and co-author of the middle school band and orchestra curriculum. She is the founder of Modern Maestro, Inc., and Palmer Research Group. Her research areas are social and cultural capital, social justice, anti-racism, and culturally relevant and responsive pedagogies. Palmer has led professional developments for the Maryland Music Educators Association, Maryland State Department of Education's Fine Arts Office, and Association for Black Women Band Directors. Her research is published in *Update: Applications of Research in Music Education.* The Palmer Research Group is a 2022 grantee for the Society for Research in Music Education.

Jocelyn A. Stevens is Associate Professor of music education at Truman State University in Kirksville, Missouri, where she oversees the Music Masters of Arts in Education program, teaches conducting, research, hip-hop, music psychology, music education courses, and supervises intern teachers. She earned a BME from Butler University, an MM in wind conducting and an MA in music education from the University of Minnesota, and a DMA in music education from the University of Georgia. Her research interests include music teacher education, mentoring, popular music pedagogy, and rural music education.

Lauren Kapalka Richerme is Associate Professor of music education at the Jacobs School of Music at Indiana University where she teaches undergraduate and graduate courses on philosophy, sociology, and cultural diversity as well as mentors graduate students' research. Lauren's publications include the philosophy book *Complicating, Considering, and Connecting Music Education*, the co-authored book *Music Education Research: An Introduction*, 24 peer reviewed articles, and 5 invited book chapters. Lauren currently serves as the editor for *Action, Criticism, and Theory in Music Education.* Prior to her university teaching, Lauren taught high school and middle school band and general music in Massachusetts.

Jason Vodicka is Associate Dean in the Rider University College of Arts and Sciences and Associate Professor of music education at Westminster Choir College of Rider University. An active author, conductor, educator, and clinician, he has presented at national and international conferences on choral music and music education, and his writing can be found in publications such as *The Choral Journal*, *The Oxford Handbook of Choral Pedagogy*, and *Update: Applications of Research in Music Education.*

Jill Wilson is Associate Professor and Coordinator of the Music Education program at Luther College in Decorah. She earned a doctorate in music education from Boston University. Current research interests include music teacher education program curricula, popular music pedagogy, dispositions, and music literacy pedagogy. Peer-reviewed research publications includethe *Journal of Research in Music Education*, *Research Issues in Music Education*,*Gender Research in Music Education*, *Visions of Research in Music Education*, *Arts Education Policy Review*, *Choral Journal*, and the*Journal of Music Teacher Education.*

1 Introduction

The Need for Disruption

Marshall Haning

"Disruption" is a word that often carries a negative connotation. It conveys a sense of things going wrong, of plans interrupted, of progress gone astray. For the most part, music teachers try to avoid things that are disruptive – things that might cause interruptions to our teaching and disorder our careful planning. When we minimize or eliminate the disruptive elements of our environment, we can take increased comfort in the quiet functioning of a normal, predictable routine.

As we move ever deeper into the 21st century, however, it has become increasingly apparent that much of what is predictable and routine about our society may not really be comfortable at all. While in earlier times the unremarked continuation of the status quo may have been regarded as the best possible outcome, today we have come to recognize that such a continuation helps to perpetuate the challenges and inequities of the past. In light of this realization, the idea of disruption – interruption, opposition, and alteration of our expected norms – may emerge as a force for positive change. Through this lens, disruption allows us to question our accepted and traditional practices, and provides an opportunity for us to change those practices when we find that they no longer represent our best approach.

In this collection, we provide examples of points in the music education curriculum that are ripe for disruption. As we grapple with the need for change in our teaching approaches and materials, and as we work to define the ongoing trajectory of our profession, opportunities for disruption may help to guide our path toward a better musical education for all students.

DOI: 10.4324/9781003410645-1

The Need for Change

Any cursory reading of the literature reveals that challenges to the status quo in music education are far from novel. For decades, teachers, scholars, and others associated with music education have argued for changes in the structure and content of our music classes. These appeals have pervaded major conferences and publications in the field of music education for at least the past 50 years, stretching from the Tanglewood Symposium to the CMS Manifesto and beyond. Articles outlining similar ideas in our practitioner journals may be even better known; papers by Kratus (2007) and Williams (2011) discussing the challenges inherent in traditional music education curricula are among the most cited works in the field.

Despite these repeated calls for change, however, our current music education curriculum continues to be strongly driven by tradition and the replication of existing structures. Large ensemble courses – primarily traditional bands, choirs, and orchestras – remain by far the most common music courses offered at the secondary level (Matthews & Koner, 2017). This continued reliance on large performing ensembles may also be indicative of the ongoing hegemony of traditional music teaching practices. For example, Allsup and Benedict (2008) recognized an "overwhelming reliance on tradition" driving the structure and curriculum of collegiate wind bands. This reliance on tradition is strongly present at all levels of music education.

Perhaps as a result, some scholars have suggested that music education is becoming increasingly disconnected from the ways in which people experience music outside of school (Jones, 2008; Kratus, 2007; Williams, 2011). Jones (2008), for example, found a wide discrepancy between the instruments that are most commonly sold and played in America and the instruments that are emphasized in music teacher education programs. While music teacher education programs continue to emphasize traditional orchestral instruments, the most commonly sold and played instruments are harmonizing instruments such as keyboard and guitar. Jones (2008) concluded that collegiate music education programs appear to be preparing students to "maintain the status quo" (p. 9) of music education rather than responding to the musical needs of today's society.

Some scholars have begun to use frameworks originally created for the analysis of dominant and impositional cultural ideologies to critique music education's reliance on tradition. Regelski (1998), for example, outlined a number of ways in which Critical Theory can be used to critique the dominant pedagogical model in music education. Like many other culturally dominant institutions, Regelski (1998) suggested that the field of music education exhibits the following characteristics:

> Taken for granted paradigms that generate equally taken for granted practices and values; legitimation procedures that advocate the institution's existence when actual results fall short of claimed values; proselytizing machinery for attracting, then initiating new conscripts; a historicity of approved practices that are passed on as "good" and accepted unthinkingly by conscripts as received wisdom; and, of course, experts who function as "managers" of the institutional knowledge base, guardians and defenders of the status quo, and gatekeepers for controlling admission.
>
> ("Methodolatry," para. 1)

In response to this hegemony of traditional ideas, Regelski (1998) suggested that music teachers should apply the principles of Critical Theory to evaluate any standardized method or teaching approach in light of its actual results. Without this critical consciousness, Regelski argued, music teachers often become more focused on the implementation of methods they unquestioningly assume to be "good" than on the observable results of those methods.

Regelski (1998) called this devotion to specific approaches to music teaching "methodolatry" – a term that is perhaps as good as any to describe the ways in which our field often seems to cling to its traditions regardless of their outcomes.

Other scholars have taken an even more critical position regarding the ways in which many traditional approaches to music education impose a set of accepted practices on teachers and students. Allsup and Benedict (2008) and Wall and Wall (2016) went so far as to position the music education curriculum as a structure of oppression, describing the traditional band classroom in particular as "an environment of learned helplessness" (Allsup & Benedict, 2008, p. 170). By applying methods of analysis and critique that have become an increasingly important part of our cultural consciousness, these authors may provide new avenues for re-evaluating the traditional music education curriculum.

It is important to recognize that not all music education scholars agree with the need for radical change in our approach to music teaching. Despite the growing number of authors who have offered passionate critiques of the current state of the music education profession, other scholars have resisted calls for a dramatic reimagining of our curriculum. These writers have urged music educators and music teacher educators to adopt a more measured approach in making changes to the traditional structures of the profession. For example, Miksza (2013) argued that "radical, sweeping changes in institutional structures have been shown time and again to be a poor approach to educational reform" (p. 49). More recently, Austin (2021) noted that "innovation has an intoxicating nature that leads many to mistake novelty as progress" (p. 8). An unquestioning rush to reform, according to these authors, may cause problems no less profound than those often ascribed to an unquestioning commitment to the status quo. Despite these calls for caution, however, almost all scholars – including those who argue against dramatic innovation – support at least measured changes and additions to existing curricular structures (Miksza, 2013; Austin, 2021; Wall, 2017; Weidner, 2019; Morrison & Demorest, 2012).

Beginnings of Disruption

In recent years, scholars have proposed a variety of ways to interrogate and modify traditional practices in music education. These approaches provide music educators and music teacher educators with important questions to ask and may lead to key disruptions of the historical status quo. In some cases, authors have focused on ways to reframe the large ensemble model to better support students' independent and creative musicianship (i.e., Haning, 2020; Morrison & Demorest, 2012; Wall, 2017; Weidner, 2019). The College Band Directors National Association (CBDNA) adopted this approach in their response to the CMS Manifesto, suggesting that "the large ensemble is currently in a position to act as a trunk from which branches of an integrative approach – including smaller groups of musicians and individuals – grow outward in a wide reach of creative and recreative musical experiences" (Peltz, 2017, p. 9). Other authors have emphasized the need to reimagine our traditional models in a more comprehensive way in order to create more inclusive classrooms (i.e., Culp & Salvador, 2021; DeLorenzo & Silverman, 2016; Edgar, 2013; Salvador et al., 2020; Siuty, 2019). These disruptions may take place on a variety of scales, but they all represent potential ways to break down cycles of replication across the profession.

At a more granular level, researchers have highlighted a variety of specific models of disruption in both the K-12 and collegiate settings. For example, Kruse (2016) described ways to use hip-hop music as both a bridge and a lens to drive new avenues of learning in the music classroom. Blackwell and Roseth (2018) showed that novel curricular structures such as problem-based learning could be used in a woodwind methods course. Weidner (2019) explored the use of participatory curricula in music teacher education programs. Finally, Haning (2020) and Hedgecoth (2018) demonstrated the effectiveness of student-directed learning models in both K-12 and collegiate ensemble settings. These examples help to illustrate both specific ways in which music educators can challenge traditional practices and how the overall process of disruption may take place. While the process of disruption is never easy, these models show that it can lead to remarkable benefits for students, teachers, and other stakeholders.

The Way Forward

At this point in our profession's history, it seems impossible to dispute that some level of disruption is necessary. As noted above, while scholars may disagree on the extent of the changes that need to be made to the music education curriculum, nearly all scholars support at least incremental changes and additions. Researchers have shown that innovative and disruptive curricular models are being implemented successfully in a variety of settings across the United States and around the world. Further, the current body of literature suggests that these disruptive practices can have positive results. While calls for change in the music education curriculum are certainly not new, it seems possible that support for these changes may be reaching a "critical mass" in the profession.

One challenge in implementing innovative and disruptive approaches to music education curricula is the difficulty of locating information about the processes of disruption and about specific curricular models that may help to challenge the status quo. Although a variety of research on these topics has been and continues to be published, it is often framed in ways that make it challenging to find or apply in a variety of contexts. Further, practicing music teachers and curriculum-makers at the K-12 level may not have reliable access to the scholarly journals where this research is often found. This book (and its companion volume) are an attempt to bring together a variety of ideas and models for disruption in the music education curriculum and provide a centralized resource for those hoping to find ways to disrupt the status quo in their own settings. This text contains descriptions of a number of potential points for disruption in our curriculum – points where the normal course of our activities can be interrupted and cycles of replication can be challenged and potentially replaced.

It is very important to note that this text is not intended to be a comprehensive listing of every possible point for disruption in the curriculum. There are many, many important conversations taking place in our classrooms, in our higher education institutions, and in our society at large regarding the ways in which our habitual patterns may be problematic and worthy of replacement. We as editors do not intend to privilege particular models or points of view through their inclusion in these books, nor do we intend to suggest that models of disruption that are not included here are in any way less important or worthy of attention. The ideas contained in these books represent only a few examples of the ways in which music educators can challenge the status quo of our music education curriculum. We offer these books as a way to begin and support a much broader range of conversations, and we look forward to learning more about the innumerable models of disruption that we were not able to include here.

This text may be used by curriculum makers throughout the educational system – teachers, professors, program coordinators, arts supervisors, and anyone else who makes curricular decisions related to music education – to identify places where they might be able to make adjustments to their own traditional practices. Anyone who makes decisions about what content should be included in a music classroom is a curriculum maker, and we encourage each and every one of them to carefully consider what parts of their curricula may be worthy of disruption. These changes do not need to be dramatic; even small steps, within a single classroom, can have a large impact (Salvador et al., 2020). In many ways, it is the act of engaging in disruption, rather than the scope of that disruption, that is most important.

Chapter Overview

This book, the first of two volumes, contains five chapters focusing on systemic disruptions that may help to move the profession of music education forward. While the second volume will be focused on disruptions that can be implemented by individual teachers or teacher educators, the chapters in this book take a broader view of disruption in our profession. As noted above, these chapters are not intended to provide a comprehensive view of all possible points of disruption in music education, but rather to serve as examples for how we might think about breaking cycles of replication in our practice.

In the first chapter, Lauren Kapalka Richerme explores approaches to rhizomatic learning – the process of growing in a variety of directions and in non-linear ways. Using her own experiences as an example and grounding those experiences in the research literature, Richerme proposes an "exit-based" positionality for music educators. This positionality encourages music teachers to identify their core values, but also to be aware of potential "exits" from those values, or ways in which they might use those values as a departure point to discover new roads to travel. Richerme argues that teachers should use their awareness of these exits to facilitate diverse and divergent growth in their ways of thinking and teaching; growing in all directions at once, as a rhizome does. To close this thought-provoking chapter, Richerme describes the ways in which utopian demands can be used to frame the need for change in music education. While the ideas presented here may be novel to many music educators, they represent a truly unique look at how we might challenge the status quo and move forward in unexpected ways.

Elizabeth S. Palmer, Jason Vodicka, Tina Huynh, Christine D'Alexander, and Lisa Crawford present a Framework for Culturally Relevant and Responsive Music Teaching (FCRRMT), which is designed to support anti-racist and socially just practices in the music classroom. Palmer et al. begin with an overview of research on anti-racism in music education, focusing on how the White Racial Frame that has historically shaped music education and classical music practices disenfranchises students and musicians of color. The authors make a strong argument for the necessity of new approaches to social justice across the music education profession, especially with regard to repertoire and music assessments and competitions. To help address these issues, Palmer et al. present a framework for music teaching that is anchored to Gloria Ladson-Billings's tenets of culturally relevant pedagogy. Through the four quadrants of their FCRRMT (teacher competencies, informed choices, authenticity, and holistic/comparative lessons), the authors construct a "counter-frame" that provides an important site for disruption of the hegemonic cultural canons that have long shaped music education.

Next, Amanda R. Draper examines the possibility of disrupting ableist viewpoints and structures in music education through the application of Universal Design for Learning (UDL) principles. Draper challenges the idea of "inclusion" in music education, arguing that this approach requires students who are labeled as having a disability to remediate perceived deficits in order to participate. Instead, she encourages music educators to recognize that disability is a social construct, and that it is up to music educators to deconstruct boundaries that prevent all students from participating fully in a musical education. By integrating UDL principles more fully into preservice teacher preparation, Draper argues, music teacher educators can influence not only the perspectives of their own students, but also the perspectives of their students' future students and beyond.

Jocelyn A. Stevens and Jill Wilson present a research study centered on the practices and approaches used by school administrators when they are hiring K-12 music teachers. These authors examined music teacher job postings in five Midwestern states, interviewed principals to provide a more in-depth understanding of their hiring practices, and finally used these results to construct a nationwide survey of school administrators. Their findings suggest that hiring practices help to reinforce the status quo of K-12 music course offerings, as principals often prioritize candidates who can effectively teach traditional courses such as band, orchestra, and choir. Based on their data, the authors are able to provide additional insight into administrators' thoughts and feelings about the hiring process. As a result, they provide important suggestions for ways in which this hiring process could be disrupted to help move the profession forward.

Finally, Daniel C. Johnson proposes a new way of approaching professional development for music educators. Johnson notes that traditional professional development sessions in music education often face challenges related to relevance, engagement, and teacher buy-in. Through a review of existing literature on professional development, Johnson clearly shows both the shortcomings of existing approaches and research-based best practices for improving the effectiveness of professional development. He then provides a clear set of recommendations for creating more relevant and teacher-centered professional development opportunities, framed through five "layers of relevance" that designers can use to improve the impact of their sessions.

Being Disruptive

Each chapter contains suggestions for breaking cycles of replication in music education, and outlines how readers can take action to implement novel curricular approaches in their own practice. Although the ideas in this book are generally larger than an individual teacher or classroom, each individual teacher, administrator, or curriculum designer has the ability to take one small step to challenge the status quo. Small changes made by individuals are the building blocks of the larger changes that so many have called for in our field. We hope that the suggestions contained in this book will encourage music teachers and other stakeholders to find ways to be disruptive in their own spheres of influence. Far from the negative connotations that normally come with that term, these disruptions have the potential to create powerful positive changes that spread beyond a single classroom or program. In addition, the suggestions and ideas presented here may suggest other possible avenues for disruption, growing from the text in divergent and unexpected ways like the rhizomatic structures described by Richerme. As you read this text, we encourage you to ask yourself: "What parts of my practice are in need of disruption? What do I take for granted in my teaching or my classroom? What kinds of growth might result from a disturbance of the status quo?" Calls for change have resonated through our profession for a century or more, with little result. With this book, we hope to provide not only a set of ideas, but clear pathways to put those ideas into action and create the change that we have been discussing for so long.

References

Allsup, R. E., & Benedict, C. (2008). The problems of band: An inquiry into the future of instrumental music education. *Philosophy of Music Education Review*, *16*(2), 156–173.

Austin, J. R. (2021). Disruptions and an event horizon for music teacher education. *Journal of Music Teacher Education*, *30*(3), 7–10. https://doi.org/10.1177/10570837211022421

Blackwell, J. A., & Roseth, N. E. (2018). Problem-based learning in a woodwind methods course: An action research study. *Journal of Music Teacher Education*, *28*(1), 55–69. https://doi.org/10.1177/1057083718769262

Culp, M. E., & Salvador, K. (2021). Music teacher education program practices: Preparing teachers to work with diverse learners. *Journal of Music Teacher Education, 30*(2), 51–64. https://doi.org/10.1177/1057083720984365

DeLorenzo, L. C., & Silverman, M. (2016). From the margins: The underrepresentation of Black and Latino students/teachers in music education. *Visions of Research in Music Education, 27*. https://opencommons.uconn.edu/vrme/vol27/iss1/3/

Edgar, S. N. (2013). Introducing social emotional learning to music education professional development. *Update: Applications of Research in Music Education, 31*(2), 28–36. https://doi.org/10.1177/8755123313480508

Haning, M. (2020). "I didn't know I could do that!" Student and teacher perceptions of an independent choral choral music learning project. *Update: Applications of Research in Music Education, 39*(2), 15–24. https://doi.org/10.1177/8755123320961083

Hedgecoth, D. M. (2018). Student perspectives and learning outcomes from self-guided ensemble rehearsal. *Research and Issues in Music Education, 14*(1). https://commons.lib.jmu.edu/rime/vol14/iss1/5/

Jones, P. M. (2008). Preparing music teachers for change: broadening instrument class offerings to foster lifewide and lifelong musicing. *Visions of Research in Music Education, 12*. https://opencommons.uconn.edu/vrme/vol12/iss1/3

Kratus, J. (2007). Music education at the tipping point. *Music Educators Journal, 94*(2), 42–48. https://doi.org/10.1177/002743210709400209

Kruse, A. J. (2016). Toward hip-hop pedagogies for music education. *International Journal of Music Education, 34*(2), 247–260. https://doi.org/10.1177/0255761414550535

Matthews, W. K., & Koner, K. (2017). A survey of elementary and secondary music educators' professional background, teaching responsibilities and job satisfaction in the United States. *Research and Issues in Music Education, 13*(1). Retrieved from http://ir.stthomas.edu/rime/vol13/iss1/2

Miksza, P. (2013). The future of music education: Continuing the dialogue about curricular reform. *Music Educators Journal, 99*(4), 45–50. https://doi.org/10.1177/0027432113476305

Morrison, S. J., & Demorest, S. M. (2012). Once from the top: Reframing the role of the conductor in ensemble teaching. In G. E. McPhereson & G. F. Welch (Eds.), *The Oxford handbook of music education* (Vol. 1, pp. 826–843). Oxford University Press.

Peltz, C. (2017). A position paper by the CBDNA music education committee. College Band Directors National Association. www.cbdna.org/wp-content/uploads/2019/09/CBDNA-The-Call-for-Perspectives.pdf

Regelski, T. A. (1998). Critical theory and praxis: Professionalizing music education. May Day Group. www.maydaygroup.org/1998/04/critical-theory-and-praxis-professionalizing-music-education/

Salvador, K., Paetz, A. M., & Tippetts, M. M. (2020). "We all have a little more work to do:" A constructivist grounded theory of transformative learning processes for practicing music teachers encountering social justice. *Journal of Research in Music Education*, *68*(2), 193–215. https://doi.org/10.1177/0022429420920630

Siuty, M. B. (2019). Teacher preparation as interruption or disruption? Understanding identity (re)constitution for critical inclusion. *Teaching and Teacher Education*, *81*, 38–49. https://doi.org/10.1016/j.tate.2019.02.008

Wall, M. P. (2017). Does school band kill creativity? *Music Educators Journal*, *105*(1), 51–56. https://doi.org/10.1177/0027432118787001

Wall, M. P. & Wall, J. K. (2016). Improvising to learn: A democratic framework for music education. In L. C. Lorenzo (Ed.), *Giving voice to democracy in music education: Diversity and social justice* (pp. 123–137). Routledge.

Weidner, B. N. (2019). Shrinking the director: Reconceptualizing ensembles in undergraduate music education. *New Directions in Music Education, 4*. www.newdirectionsmsu.org/issue-4-special-focus-issue-imte2019/weidner/

Williams, D. A. (2011). The elephant in the room. *Music Educators Journal*, *98*(1), 51–57. https://doi.org/10.1177/0027432111415538

2 Locate the Nearest Exit

Refrains, Rhizomes, and Utopian Demands

Lauren Kapalka Richerme

Disrupting longstanding music education curricular practices necessitates reflection about how teachers and students position themselves in the present. This positioning often occurs by claiming where we are, either in terms of a clear point of view or a planned trajectory; one might be an LGBTQ ally or aim to promote equity. Not until an exit sign in Greece positioned me did I begin to consider the limits of such practices.

It was a warm Sunday morning in June 2017, and, en route back from the International Philosophy of Music Education Symposium, I spent a day alone in Athens. In typical Lauren fashion, I was one of the first people in line at the entrance to the Acropolis, a collection of magnificent ancient hilltop ruins. I paid my entrance fee and headed inside. As the main path diverged, instead of following the already substantial crowd of people continuing upward, I walked straight ahead, past an unmanned booth and small gate. Continuing along the trail, I read the labels on the sporadic monuments and artifacts in eerie silence.

My newfound isolation combined with a sign reading "Acropolis" made me concerned that I may have inadvertently exited the Acropolis. I thought about the prospect of arguing a security guard that I had already paid my 20 Euro admission fee; I imagined him not understanding my English and feeling embarrassed that I knew absolutely no Greek. I had a cell phone complete with a working GPS and downloaded offline map of all Athens. I could tell you exactly where on planet Earth I was. What I could not tell you was my positioning in relation to the Acropolis' artificial boundaries. While the limits of arbitrary borders could be a chapter in itself, my story took another turn.

DOI: 10.4324/9781003410645-2

Walking far below the fortified walls supporting the central ruins, I worried more and more that I had mistakenly left the park. As I began looking for another "Acropolis" sign, I came across a sign that read "Exit," with a hand-drawn arrow pointing to the left. I stared at the letters for a few moments, sensing that I had learned something, but unsure of what. "Exit," I reasoned, "That means I must still be inside the boundaries of the Acropolis."

As relief set in, I began thinking about music education and all the times I *thought* that I had exited. For instance, I have claimed to move beyond Eurocentric musical practices, colorblind pedagogies, and heteronormative language. In looking for metaphoric entrance signs affirming my progress toward these ends, had I neglected to see the exit signs indicating the persistence of problematic practices? I then thought about how this positioning reminded me of Deleuze and Guattari's (1987) concept of the refrain, which involves a central home surrounded by opportunities for exit.

In this chapter, I propose the possibilities of an exit-based positionality for music education. I begin by further problematizing music educators' positioning practices. Next, I draw on Deleuze and Guattari's concept of the refrain to offer an initial image of an exit-based positionality. I then consider possible benefits of such positioning and offer examples of such practices. Subsequently, I consider how rhizomatic motion might inform this exit-based positionality. Finally, after considering a few limitations of exit-based positionality, I posit that making utopian demands can reinvigorate the ongoing value construction key to music educators' positioning processes.

From Why? to What?

It can be tempting for music teacher educators who aim to challenge teachers' and students' current positionality to begin by asking them why they engage in their current practices. For example, teacher educators might question: "Why do you feel at home with some musical practices and not others? Why do you identify as a performer but not a composer?" Former FBI hostage negotiator Voss (2016) explains the limits of such inquires, arguing that "Why?" questions can backfire. He writes: "Regardless of what language the word 'why' is translated into, it's accusatory" (p. 153). In other words, by implying that one's present position is problematic, asking "Why?" invokes a sort of defensiveness that can discourage changed action. Moreover,

Voss argues that addressing "Why?" questions involves rationality, which, particularly in hostage situations, does not necessarily drive humans' actions.

Instead, Voss (2016) advocates repeatedly asking "What?" the hostage taker values. By diving into the often irrational desires that guide actions, negotiators can formulate futures that honor those values, freeing hostages in the process. While music teacher education obviously differs from hostage negotiation, human action in many contexts derives not from logic but from individuals' cherished values. For example, Lakoff (2004) argues that people don't necessarily vote what is in their personal best interest. Instead, as demonstrated by the iconic Barack Obama "Hope" campaign poster, they vote their identities, and they vote their values. As such, rationalizing why music educators might interrogate their present positionality may have little impact on their actions.

The tension between asking "Why are you here?" and "What do you value here?" creates a dilemma. Focusing on "Why?" invokes defensiveness, but it enables the educative reflection that can inspire different futures. Alternatively, while asking "What do you value here?" avoids defensiveness, it draws attention only to the present, thus inhibiting the possibilities of changed futures. This illustrates the need for understandings about positionality attentive to both present and future without encouraging defensiveness. Deleuze and Guattari (1987) focus on abstract forces rather than socially constructed values, but their concept of the "refrain" may serve as a starting place for such imaginings.

Refrains

Although people typically think of musical refrains in terms of similarity, Deleuze and Guattari (1987) conceive of their concept of the "refrain" as interconnected with difference and differing as much as with similarity. They describe the refrain as having three "aspects." First, the refrain has a center: a calm, stable home "in the heart of chaos" (p. 311). In music education, a value such as hard work or a practice such as creativity might constitute this center.

The defined space surrounding the center constitutes the second part of the refrain: its territory. This territory, or what Grosz (2008) calls a "yard," (p. 52), occurs through the use of "landmarks and marks of all kinds" to select and separate the ordered interior from the chaos existing beyond the circle (Deleuze & Guattari, 1987, p. 311). Like the fences, curbs, or line of trees that demarcate property boundaries, the yard protects the center. Applying Deleuze's refrain to music education, Gould (2012) explains that music educators create territories through repeated music performance conventions, musical skills, and pedagogies. While these practices might vary slightly from year to year, their general predictability forms familiar yards.

A third part of the refrain involves a breakaway from this organization. Deleuze and Guattari (1987) write: "One opens the circle a crack, opens it all the way, lets someone in, calls someone, or else goes out oneself, launches forth" (p. 311). As such, Deleuzian exiting involves not only endless potentialities but countless ways of exiting. This image of a center and yard attends to one's present values and practices, while the exits that surround the center and yard serve as constant reminders of future possibilities. Figure 2.1 offers a visualization of the three aspects – home, yard, and ways out – of the Deleuzian refrain.

By asking "What do you value here?" while maintaining an openness to possible exits, music educators can consider how various musical and educative practices can further their cherished values. Imagine a music educator who has focused on Orff ensembles but asserts teamwork as a primary value driving their practices. For this educator, teamwork might function as their center or home and Orff pedagogy as their territory or yard. Adding ways out or exits might

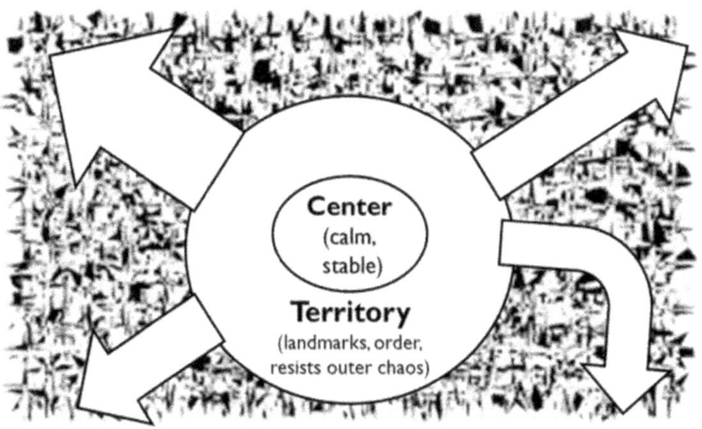

Figure 2.1 Visualization of Deleuze's Refrain.

mean that the teacher retains their emphasis on teamwork while experimenting with ukulele groups, garage bands, laptop ensembles, or any other number of practices in addition to or in place of Orff pedagogy. The home value of teamwork remains, but the exit allows the music educator to reimagine the possibilities for that value, including how it might intersect with other values. Alternatively, experimenting with various exits may enable the music educator to maintain their Orff pedagogy territory while, for instance, reimagining that territory through the center value of emotional awareness and expression.

Possibilities

Focusing on maintaining one's core values while attending to exits has four potential advantages. First, an emphasis on exits, as opposed to entrances, attends to the divergent ways that educators can live out cherished values. The word "entrance" comes from the Latin "intra" meaning within. Entrances emphasize the stability of existing within a defined area; one does not *go* within, one *is* within.

Conversely, the word exit comes from the Latin "exire," with "ex" meaning out and "ire" meaning go. The divergent motion of going out opens a world of possibilities beyond one's immediate ground. When I exited the Acropolis, I could go to another museum, to shops or restaurants in a different part of the city, or to the airport. Similarly, teachers focused on exiting consider many potential practices. Such action resists the selection of a single new music education trend absent critical deliberation about other options.

Second, an exit-based positionality reminds music educators of the gravitas involved in changing their practices. Exiting, as those involved with Brexit can attest, is a significant act. Who among us has not felt the need to double check that we have all of our belongings when passing through the giant security exit signs on the way out of an airport? Likewise, temporary or permanent exits of present music teaching and learning philosophies might incite a moment of hesitation as one considers the value-laden nature of what they leave behind. While teachers who staunchly resist altering their practices might benefit from examining what specifically they feel concerned about leaving, I increasingly see preservice and practicing teachers who will adopt the latest trend, be it Quaver Music, or Boomwackers, or Social Emotional Learning, without reflecting on what practices, and more importantly what values, they discard in the process. A positioning that attends to exits encourages teachers to hesitate and focus on how their central values might guide implementation.

A third potential advantage of an exit-based positionality is that it can encourage reflection on the limits of present practices. When I saw the exit sign at the Acropolis, I considered all of the times I claimed to have left problematic practices. While it is important that music educators celebrate improvements, such action can lead to a false sense of completeness and stability. For instance, imagine a teacher who has traditionally used music and musical practices associated with White men. What if that educator reimagines their positionality as one that honors diversity and then enacts that position by adding compositions by a couple of female and Latine composers to their repertoire?

While the teacher should take pride in those changes, an exit-based positionality would encourage them simultaneously to consider how their present practices may still inhibit diversity in all its forms. Stated differently, in addition to looking for how one's home value could inspire divergent exiting, music educators might look for exit signs indicating problems with their present practices. For instance, if an educator values inclusivity and equity, then they might question: How do my current practices still resist such aims? Upon considering this question, the educator might find that, despite their addition of a couple of female and Hispanic composers, their repertoire remained overwhelmingly comprised of White, male composers. Moreover, they might find that participation fees, after-school obligations, or other requirements served as barriers to recruiting students more representative of their school in terms of race, socioeconomic status, and other qualities. The educator might also find that their pedagogy and leadership selection favored students already privileged through private lessons and other resources, while minimizing achievement opportunities for other students.

A fourth potential advantage of an exit-based positionality is that it emphasizes the temporal nature of both physical and conceptual positioning. Imagine asking preservice or practicing teachers to take a look at the exit sign in their current room. Attending to the certainty that you and the students or teachers will all exit a room highlights the fleeting nature of our positionality within it. Such a realization can potentially make the process of exiting less overwhelming.

Yet, the decision to exit a room occurs under certain circumstances, including at a specific time. The sounding of a fire alarm may call for an immediate exit, or exit can be prolonged as students linger in conversation. While ultimately exiting is a binary decision – one does or does not exit – those contemplating exiting generally attend to the conditions that necessitate exiting. My exit from the Acropolis depended on tiring of monument-viewing, feeling overwhelmed by the increasing crowd, and needing a reprieve from the midday sun. Instead of asking *if* teachers might implement alternative practices, I wonder what might happen if teacher educators question: *When* might you do so? For example, envision if the aforementioned equity and inclusivity-focused teacher constructed a lesson plan with multiple potential points of exit. They could ponder: What verbal and gestural student actions, reactions, and omissions indicate that my lesson is undermining equity or inclusivity, and how might I exit in response? In order to emphasize divergent exits rather than convergent entrances, the teacher posit two or more possibilities for each potential exit point.

More broadly, teachers and students centering the values of equity and inclusivity might consider questions such as: When would a music educator make time for rap, Latin, or popular music–centered small groups or a social justice themed musical event? When would an ensemble attend fewer competitions? When would circumstances necessitate starting a hip-hop class or a songwriting club? Through such inquiries, the exit sign serves not as a barrier between present and future but as a reminder of the inevitable change that constitutes existence.

Additionally, focusing on *when* one might exit their current center and yard can make the present more meaningful. Hours after the Greek exit sign positioned me, I had particular trouble leaving the Acropolis. Even though I had spent ample time standing in awe at the Parthenon and other monuments, when I came within about 30 feet of the actual exit gates, I decided to turn back and linger at the nearby statues. Staring at those exit gates created a temporal opening in which I absorbed and appreciated those final images and moments in a way that I could not have otherwise done. Similarly, understanding our current practices as conscious choices that one will inevitably someday exit, rather than as accepted habits that will persist indefinitely, encourages more focused attention in the present.

Rhizomatic Motion

Considering the question "When will you exit?" necessitates that teachers understand their daily lesson plans and overarching curricula as flexible and motion-filled. Although lesson plans and curricula typically enable points of exit, how music educators and students understand their exiting process can bound or free their subsequent actions. For example, a teacher noticing an ensemble class struggling with a certain rhythmic passage may exit their planned lesson and focus on that rhythm. Yet, such an exit still leads to a largely predetermined goal of a standardized music performance. In contrast, a teacher noticing students expressing sadness over a recent world event might exit their plan by switching to a solemn piece or providing time for individual or group composition. Deleuze and Guattari's (1987) concept of the rhizome, particularly when contrasted with the image of trees, can provide further insights into these contrasting ways of exiting.

If you are unfamiliar with the term "rhizome," then you might take a moment and search for images of rhizomes on your smartphone or computer. Ginger roots will likely appear as one of the first and most frequent images. Their diverse shapes, sizes, and growth patterns reveal that ginger and other botanical rhizomes grow unpredictably. Unlike anchored, vertically reaching trees, rhizomes' horizontal growth enables them to shoot off into divergent directions. Additionally, while trees retain a certain order and hierarchy, with leaves and buds emerging at prescribed points, the rhizome can send up shoots freely at unexpected points (May, 2005).

Similar to plant rhizomes, Deleuze and Guattari (1987) explain their abstract concept of the rhizome as having "neither beginning nor end, but always a middle *(milieu)* from which it grows and which it overspills" (p. 21). They add that rhizomes continually connect with diverse ideas, objects, and practices, writing "any point of a rhizome can be connected to anything other, and must be" (p. 7). The act of scanning the various images of rhizomes on an electronic device is one form of rhizomatic motion. Clicking randomly through the various links may connect a wandering viewer to information ranging from cooking rhizomes to gardening tips to artists' webpages.

In the example above, the teacher who abandoned their lesson plan only to focus on rhythm exited in a tree-like manner. They had a hierarchical end goal, and though deviating from their familiar home plan, they moved along a clear, mostly predictable trajectory. In contrast, the teacher who switched to a solemn piece or individual or group composition project in response to students' expressed sadness, exited rhizomatically. The exit served students' emotional needs in the moment, rather than the needs of an upcoming performance or other predetermined aim. Like a botanical rhizome connecting to whatever objects or life-forms cross its divergent paths, the imagined teacher's rhizomatic exit bridged divides between school and societal events as well as between students' affective states and class content.

In asking to what extent musical and pedagogical exits are rhizomatic versus tree-like, teachers and students might consider whether their actions aim toward a destination. Deleuze and Guattari (1987) write: "The tree imposes the verb 'to be,' but the fabric of the rhizome is the conjunction, 'and ...and ...and ...'" (p. 25). Teachers and students focusing on rhizomatic motion might ask: Does this diversion from a plan lead to a more solidified understanding of music making, self, and communal engagements, or does it lead to more possibilities for connection, uncertainty, and divergent interpretations and processes, including in relation to social justice and other key values?

There are countless ways that teachers and students can exit lesson plans through rhizomatic motion. Perhaps a student's question about a style of music leads to a historical investigation of its relationship with local folk traditions, perhaps including how such traditions may have propagated sexist, racist, or other problematic hierarchies. Maybe the teacher extends this focus on equity by initiating a discussion about who and what scholars have traditionally included and excluded in such a genre, and subsequently to an exploration of inclusions and exclusions in society more broadly. Alternatively, maybe a student's playful variation on a musical theme becomes the impetus for group improvisation, and then group composition, and then the adding of electronic samples and equity-promoting video clips to accompany the composition, and so on.

More broadly, a rhizomatic exit from one's current curricula might involve opportunities for greater inclusivity by connecting with different school subjects or community groups, or maybe it fosters equity through free-flowing experiments across musical genres and practices. Perhaps the exit also troubles existing divides between class labels such as "chorus," "music technology," and "general music." Conversely, a tree-like exit from one's curricula might involve bringing in a specialist on the style of music currently under investigation. In such moments, current musical practices serve as roots that ground the trunk and branches of added musical expertise in that area.

Although Deleuze and Guattari (1987) favor rhizomatic over tree-like motion, they ultimately encourage ongoing alternation and integration of the two. They describe, "A new rhizome may form in the heart of a tree, the hollow of a root, the crook of a branch" (p. 15), and elsewhere note: "Trees have rhizome lines, and the rhizome points of arborescence" (p. 34). Imagine ginger roots intermingling with the roots and branches of multiple trees. As the trees grow vertically, they may dislodge and reconfigure the ginger; as the ginger grows horizontally, it might connect with other parts of the same tree or different trees as well as nearby power lines, buildings, or other entities.

Drawing on this image, one way that music teacher educators might experiment with intersections of tree-like and rhizomatic motion could involve picking a few points of exit on a standard lesson plan. While lesson plans tend to function like trees, with clear aims and each part serving a preset function, the exits could favor rhizomatic motion, as well as occasional new branches. Perhaps at each exit point, students provide three or four options. Growing from the central goals of inclusivity and equity, two or three of those exits could involve rhizomatic connections, perhaps to different subjects, world events, styles of music, and contemporary music practices. Additionally, one of those exits could involve tree-like growth, such as another potential way to practice the concept (e.g., dynamics) at hand.

Students could repeat the same practice with curricular plans. For instance, a teacher focused on inclusivity might rhizomatically exit an existing curriculum by encouraging students to seek out, experiment with, reinterpret, and integrate various genres of music as well as create their own unique music styles, practices, and products. When a student shows curiosity about a specific genre or practice, the educator might plan options for tree-like growth that guides the student's engagement with key characteristics and goals within such boundaries. Subsequently, the educator might rhizomatically exit that new curriculum, perhaps encouraging students to experiment with different musical and life connections. In short, in addition to providing opportunities for exits from preset practices, lesson plans, and curricula, teachers and students might specifically experiment with exiting through rhizomatic motion.

Limitations

A potential limitation of both rhizomatic motion and an exit-based positionality is that they can leave one's home values unquestioned. Since in the Deleuzian refrain exiting occurs in relation to one's home and yard, one's home values inform and ultimately confine the possibilities for exiting. For instance, an educator who does not currently see any value in social justice, creative personal expression, or connections with local music communities drastically restricts possible points of exit. While experimenting with various exits may encourage the teacher to trade their current home values for social justice or other aims, such action need not necessarily occur.

Particular kinds of musical and educative practices may also serve as key values in and of themselves, thus closing off significant potential exits; valuing rap, classical guitar, or bluegrass fiddling de-centers other possible ways of being and becoming musical. In short, values are always relational and exclusionary. How, then, might music educators continually reconsider their home values?

Deleuze and Guattari (1987) suggest that the process of exiting can contribute to the alteration of one's home and yard. They write that while individuals might return to their familiar center and territory after exiting, "No one will recognize us any more when we come back" (p. 191). As such, exiting might serve not only as a respite from present centers and yards but as a lens through which individuals analyze and perhaps reimagine them. However, since logic does not always drive individuals' values, music educators might need more than personal reflection to jostle long-held beliefs and self-conceptions.

Dialoguing with others can serve as a starting point for questioning one's own values. Yet, how often does one leave a conversation or even a conference or professional development opportunity with altered values? Sometimes this occurs because the dialogue centers on *why* music teachers have yet to change their practices, thus invoking the defensiveness described above. However, even when music educators meaningfully debate *what* they might value, they may have trouble envisioning significantly different ways forward.

Deleuze and Guattari (1987) challenge readers to push the limits of the present through exploring markedly different futures, or what some might call utopias. Parr (2008) explains that for Deleuze, "Utopian thought consists of an experimental struggle with the past taking place in the context of the present, all for the sake of the future" (p. 48). Consistent with Deleuze and Guattari's emphasis on difference and differing, utopias are neither static nor singular. As such, music educators need not one vision of utopia but many utopian imaginings.

Dialoguing about multiple possible utopias has the potential to unsettle one's current central values and accompanying familiar practices. When used to complement Deleuze and Guattari's (1987) concepts of the refrain and rhizomatic motion, utopian visioning can foster a productive tension within one's present center or home. For example, imagining utopias in which students currently underrepresented in music classes, such as those from lower socio-economic status backgrounds, played a key role in one's program could encourage a teacher to trade their current central home value of discipline for the value of inclusion. This does not mean that discipline would play no role on that teacher's utopia, but such visioning would trouble instances when centering discipline excludes certain individuals.

Any one utopia or even group of utopias, however, can encourage tree-like motion. For instance, a teacher who thoroughly envisions what an inclusion-centered music education would look like might make all of their exiting serve that end, thus largely solidifying that aim and resisting other values and practices. While the teacher and students might deem the inclusion-centered practices preferable to past actions, they might miss other meaningful exits and rhizomatic journeys.

Alternatively, numerous, constantly-changing utopias have little hope of significantly troubling current practices. This relates to a longstanding critique of Deleuze and Guattari's work, as well as that of other poststructuralist thinkers. Alcoff (1988) explains that when poststructuralist authors call for total difference and ongoing differing, such as that needed for rhizomatic wandering, they make gender and other qualities invisible and thus undercut the ability to oppose dominant structures and practices. For example, the music educator who centers the inclusion of diverse individual students, but who does not name the various categories of students currently excluded from their program, may omit attention to the socioeconomic structures that encouraged those exclusions in the first place.

Furthermore, since even small changes to longstanding habits can feel overwhelming, music educators who espouse a reimagined value system might only make incremental alterations to their lesson plans and curricula. For instance, music educators claiming to value inclusivity may initially add short-term, unrefined composition exercises to their classes. While small changes are often a necessary starting point, music educators may come to understand them as sufficient, thus undermining their own expressed values. There is no easy solution to habitual entrenchment, but part of markedly disrupting present practices can involve setting clear goals for change.

Given the limits of both solidified utopian imaginings and aimless wandering, music educators might combine aspects of utopian visioning with the naming of specific problems and significant goals. Such action balances tree-like fixity that can encourage substantial changes to practice with a rhizomatic variability that can leave open divergent ways forward. Such a process shares similarities with what Weeks (2011) explains as a utopian demand.

Before addressing utopian demands, the idea of utopias, including their potential relationships with present practices and circumstances, needs further explanation. Since utopias play only a minimal role in Deleuze and Guattari's philosophy, I complement their work with that of other authors who emphasize the possibilities of disrupting present boundaries and practices.

Utopian Demands

Ranciere (2017) distinguishes between two classic definitions of utopia. In one sense, utopia involves "a simple negation of reality, a work of pure theory or imagination" (p. 219). While such creativity can provide insights and inspiration, Weeks (2011) problematizes that traditional utopian novels "suspend history" (p. 210). She adds that by both avoiding conflict within their described worlds and resisting unexpected developments, such authors tend toward a closure that readers may interpret as a "state of impossible perfection" (p. 210).

Alternatively, Ranciere (2017) explains a second sense of utopia, which, rather than negating "reality," negates "the present" (p. 219). He writes that such a utopia "makes visible present reality as nonnecessary and another reality as possible" (p. 219). Weeks (2011) clarifies that utopias go beyond just "better visions of the present;" rather, they involve "visions of radically different worlds" (p. 196). She continues: "By estranging us from the engrossing familiarity of the everyday, the utopian form can provide us with a standpoint in the new from which to assess the present critically" (p. 205). It follows that utopian visions may provide the distance needed to trouble one's home music education values. Given the limits of detailed utopian novels, how might teachers and students go about imagining such utopias?

Weeks (2011) argues for the possibilities of what she calls "utopian demands," which she explains "must constitute a radical and potentially far-reaching change, generate critical distance, and stimulate the political imagination" (p. 221). Utopian demands occur in the present while pointing toward a break from it that is substantial enough to "raise eyebrows" (p. 220). By expressing a single immediate desire, utopian demands enable multiple forms of political mobilization toward that aim. As such, Weeks describes utopian demands as suggesting "a direction rather than a destination" (p. 221). Practically speaking, utopian demands enable music educators to make a single significant statement that may unsettle their own and others' home values prior to constructing a comprehensive plan for implementation. This recalls a quotation by E. L. Doctorow who, comparing writing to driving at night in the fog, observed: "You can only see as far as your headlights, but you can make the whole trip that way" (as cited in Heller, 2018, p. 16). While a teacher need not know exactly how they will go about enacting their utopian demand, they should have enough metaphoric light to illuminate their next step, be it a dialogue, reading, or specific experience.

Offering an example of a utopian demand, Weeks (2011) asserts that the government should provide a living wage to people, usually women, who stay home raising children and doing housework. This specific demand marks a clear break from the present, yet it remains ambiguous enough that its political enactment could take many forms. The vagueness and overuse of much current music education discourse surrounding diversity, inclusivity, and equity no longer raises eyebrows and therefore resists stimulating music educators' political imaginations.

However, the profession has the potential to reframe such statements as utopian demands. These might include: Less than 25% of all repertoire on every concert will come from musical canons, including not only the Western classical canon but the canons created through Kodaly, Orff, and other methodologies as well as one's own canon of repertoire. Perhaps such exiting of one's familiar musical canon could encourage a teacher to experiment rhizomatically with student creativity, local music making, or music from historically marginalized global communities. As this example demonstrates, the specificity of utopian demands serves a key role in their potential to raise eyebrows and ultimately create change. Instead of relying on vague language, such as phrases like "more equity" or "greater diversity," utopian demands often use numeric measures, in this case limiting familiar repertoire to 25% of one's programming.

Other utopian demands that use percentages to support practices related to diversity, inclusivity, and equity might involve specific musical practices or pedagogical focuses. For example, teachers might demand that they spend at least 40% of their class time focusing on emotions, including the feelingful aspects of music making as well as students' emotions, or they might demand a minimum of 35% of their lessons on creativity. What if, rather than defaulting to the right versus wrong performances and singular answers typical in many music classrooms, music educators demanded that they spend at least 25% of their time on the ambiguous and complex nature of musical experiences. Alternatively, they might demand spending 10% of their time explaining the systems of privilege and oppression that ground their selected genres, practices, and repertoire. By naming a specific comparison as a metric for one's progress, these utopian demand resists teachers, students, and policymakers understanding vague proclamations or minimal changes as sufficient.

In addition to percentages, utopian demands might also center values by inverting current relationships. Consider the utopian demand: State music educators associations and other institutions will provide greater resources and recognition to efforts aimed at improving equitable access to music education than to those focused on musical achievements. While such a statement does not necessitate foregoing recognition of musical achievements, it reverses the typical relationship between the values of equity and musical success.

Similarly, imagine a utopian demand in which a music educator vowed to spend more time and resources on students from lower socioeconomic status backgrounds than on students from higher socioeconomic class backgrounds. While many music educators devote the majority of their curricular elective time and outside of school mentorship to the latter, inverting this relationship would mean devoting more energy and resources to meeting the needs of students with the fewest financial supports. It would also involve inventing and centering music electives that attract and retain students from historically marginalized communities. Importantly, these percentages and value inversions should be both grounded in local needs and significant enough that they pull teachers far beyond their familiar practices.

In closing, positioning oneself in relation to centers, yards, and exits fosters a "You Are Here" that resists both stagnation and a single trajectory to "there." It encourages a moment of hesitation before changing one's value-laden practices and emphasizes the ongoing intersections of one's past, present, and future positionalities. By distinguishing exits that involve tree-like and rhizomatic motion and favoring the latter, music educators and students can resist situations in which exiting primarily involves preplanned, convergent aims. Additionally, through the creation of utopian demands, music educators might unsettle their present home values.

I exit this chapter by leaving readers with two questions that I currently still ponder: What problematic practices have I not left behind, and when will I exit them? How is the present nonnecessary, and what utopian changes can I imagine? Readers could also ask *what* they find valuable in this chapter, this book, and the community of people with which they read. Perhaps readers might now direct their attention to a doorway or other nearby exit and position themselves in relation to it – you are here.

References

Alcoff, L. (1988). Cultural feminism versus post-structuralism: The identity crisis in feminist theory. *Journal of Women in Culture and Society*, *13*(3), 405–446.

Deleuze, G., & Guattari, F. (1987). *A thousand plateaus: Capitalism and schizophrenia.* (B. Massumi, Trans.). University of Minnesota Press. (Original work published 1980).

Gould, E. (2012). Uprooting music education pedagogies and curricula: Becoming musician and the Deleuzian refrain. *Discourse: Studies in the Cultural Politics of Education*, *33*(1), 75–86.

Grosz, E. (2008). *Chaos, territory, art: Deleuze and the framing of the earth.* Columbia University Press.

Heller, N. (2018). The philosopher redefining equality. *The New Yorker.* www.newyorker.com/magazine/2019/01/07/the-philosopher-redefining-equality

Lakoff, G. (2004). *Don't think of an elephant! Know your values and frame the debate.* Thousand Oaks.

May, T. (2005). *Gilles Deleuze: An introduction.* Cambridge University Press.

Parr, A. (2008). *Deleuze and memorial culture*. Edinburgh University Press.

Ranciere, J. (2017). The senses and uses of utopia. In S. D. Chrostowski & J. D. Ingram (Eds.), *Political uses of utopia: New Marxist, anarchist, and radical democratic perspectives* (pp. 219–232). Columbia University Press.

Voss, C. (2016). *Never split the difference: Negotiating as if your life depended on it.* HarperCollins Publishers.

Weeks, K. (2011). *The problem of work: Feminism, Marxism, antiwork politics, and postwork imaginaries.* Duke University Press.

3 Disrupting the Status Quo

Anti-Racism, Social Justice, and Culturally Relevant and Responsive Music Teaching

Elizabeth S. Palmer, Jason Vodicka, Tina Huynh, Christine D'Alexander, and Lisa Crawford

Uncomfortable truth: The United States is a White supremacist nation.

The United States' legacy of White supremacy is the result of hundreds of years of colonialism, imperialism, broken treaties, chattel slavery, and government policies that harm historically marginalized and forgotten communities while elevating White people or Whiteness (Brayboy, 2013; Mineo, 2020; Rabaka, 2013; Young, 2021). White supremacy is so prevalent that most people do not realize when they are participating in or upholding White supremacist institutions (Feagin, 2020). PreK-12 and post-secondary music education is one manifestation of institutionalized White supremacy. Dismantling White supremacy in music education requires critical examination of musical dispositions, widely accepted norms, and curricula (Ewell, 2020).

The Framework for Culturally Relevant and Responsive Music Teaching (FCRRMT) is a mechanism that de-centers Whiteness and Eurocentric aesthetics in music, ushering in anti-racist and socially just practices in the music classroom, and eventually dismantling White supremacist ideologies in our field. FCRRMT takes into consideration the nuances of teaching music and offers pathways for teachers to develop their cultural competencies in order to better serve students with a wide range of cultural and musical backgrounds. The expansion of music curricula to encompass student-centered and culture-centered

DOI: 10.4324/9781003410645-3

teaching is a requirement for addressing White supremacy in music education (Palmer et al., 2021). This chapter positions FCRRMT as a tool for socially just and anti-racist music teaching (Palmer, 2018).

Anti-Racism in Music Education

Racism is the belief that there are inherent differences between races and that one's own race is superior to another. Kendi (2019) asserts, "racism is the marriage between racist policies and racist ideas that produce normalized inequities" (p. 18). In the United States, racist policies and racist ideas have created vast inequities among communities of color. The United States education system and, by extension, music education are rife with racialized systems of oppression (Palmer, 2018). These racialized systems include Eurocentric and patriotic-centric curriculum, district-sanctioned graded performance assessments, audition requirements, and programs that prioritize performance over creativity. These systems prioritize individuals with whom curriculum writers, school administrators, and instructional specialists consider to be the average student – a White student – while largely excluding students of color. Gellerstein (2021) notes "music education has historically and systemically marginalized generations of non-White, particularly Black students, while elevating the mythos of European artistic supremacy resulting in cultural reproduction that exclusively benefited White students" (p. 19). Elpus and Abril (2019) note that African-American and Latinx students are underrepresented in high school ensemble classes. While their research did not explain this phenomenon, it brought forth "three obvious questions: 'Is the underrepresentation of African American and Latino students in instrumental music a problem of access, a problem of appeal, or a matter of familial support? (p. 335)." These questions point to issues of social justice and racism within music education (Palmer, 2018).

Music education, and classical music generally, can be viewed through what sociologist Joe Feagin calls the White Racial Frame. The White Racial Frame is an "overarching worldview, one that encompasses important racial ideas, terms, images, emotions, and interpretations" (2020, p. 3). Feagin notes, "a particular frame structures the thinking process and shapes what people see or do not see, in important societal settings" (2020, p. 10). Music classrooms, rehearsal spaces, and performance venues are the societal and social spaces in which musicians frequently operate (Palmer, 2017). There is a set of norms or expectations for those spaces based in White supremacy.

Music theorist Phillip Ewell uses Feagin's (2020) White Racial Frame to address hegemony in the field of music theory. He states that music theory exclusively prefers Western tonal music of the Common Practice Period, creating little space in an undergraduate music curriculum to explore music from non-Western cultures or even contemporary Western music (Ewell, 2020). Similarly, Kajikawa (2019) discusses *classical music* as a "possession" and "an investment in elitism." The continued investment in classical music continues to uphold notions of acceptable aesthetics, musical intelligence, and musical thought (see O'Flynn, 2005). United States PreK-12 and post-secondary music education institutions participate in the White Racial Frame of curriculum and aesthetics by overteaching music from the Western canon; through music theory that prioritizes examples from the Common Practice Period and early 20th century; by excluding non-classical styles of music in applied study; and through music history course offerings that center art music developed in Europe. Failing to develop the competencies to create and analyze diverse musics, undergraduate music students are ill-prepared to analytically engage with music outside of the Western classical canon, much less to teach diverse musics as PreK-12 music teachers.

Defining Anti-Racism

Anti-racism is a radical approach to combating the violence of systemic racism. This concept moves beyond the ideals of race-neutral dispositions such as *color blindness* and a *post-racial* American society (see Bonilla-Silva, 2015). Anti-racism is "expressing the idea that racial groups are equal and none needs developing, and is supporting policy that reduces racial inequities" (Kendi, 2019, p. 24). An anti-racist approach to music education requires commitment to dismantling musical institutions that disenfranchise students by dismissing their musical backgrounds and ways of musicking, and those that create barriers to participation.

After *Brown v. Board of Education*, the education of students of color focused on deficit-based teaching as a means of correcting cultural disadvantages in order to prepare students to live in dominant culture (Lind & McKoy, 2016). Lind and McKoy point out that the perceived achievement gap of students of color is the result of cultural difference theories in schooling,

> Regardless of socioeconomic status, race, or ethnicity all students had rich cultures and heritages and that the academic achievement gap was a result of significant cultural conflicts in school experienced by many students in the racial minority... Anthropologists, social linguists, and educators who embraced this and similar cultural difference theories surmised that developing stronger links between students' home culture and school might result in improved academic achievement and instructional interactions.
>
> (2016, p. 13)

In reaction to these perceived inequities, culturally relevant and responsive teaching developed as an asset-based approach that prioritizes students' cultures, capitalizing on the knowledge students have gained outside of the classroom (Palmer et al., 2021).

Social Justice through Instruction and Curricula

In both the classroom and studio setting, music education in the United States has historically relied on a hierarchical teacher–student (master–apprentice) relationship (Allsup, 2016). The learning is teacher-driven: the teacher is "narrator" and the student is "listener" (Freire, 1970/2000; Palmer, 2018). Students are considered *tabula rasa*, with very little control or decision-making authority. The teacher's musical knowledge and dispositions are centered, and students' musical knowledge, experiences, and tastes remain at the margins (Palmer, 2018). Teacher-centered approaches privilege teachers and oppress students, and oppression leads to exclusion (Matthews, 2015; Palmer, 2018). In her 2020 visual album, *Black is King*, prolific artist Beyoncé says, "to live without reflection for so long might make you wonder if you truly exist." Students have the right to be heard, be seen, and *feel* seen in music classrooms. When students are not involved in the musical learning process, they are denied the opportunity to participate fully in their own growth and development. From a constructivist viewpoint, they are essentially denied an education.

In addition to teacher-driven learning, curricular choices can marginalize and exclude students. Within the broad context of music curriculum there are two issues which need to be immediately addressed in order to create an anti-racist music education. These issues are: (a) repertoire and the lack of authenticity in textbooks and published literature, and (b) performance assessments and adjudication.

Repertoire

In the early 1990s MENC (now the National Association for Music Education, or NAfME) expanded its definition of multicultural education with the intention of generating a greater understanding and appreciation of cultural diversity (Anderson, 1992). Mason (2010) surveyed music textbooks by two publishers and found there were thousands of songs featured from approximately 107 countries. While this diverse repertoire is to be commended, multicultural music education is essentially outward-facing, failing to focus on the music of the many cultures within the United States. Additionally, while students confronted music from dozens of countries, the instructional strategies remained centered in Western practices (Hess, 2015).

Authenticity of repertoire is also a concern. Though Dodd (2020) discusses authenticity regarding Western classical music, the authentic musical approaches to music outside of the Western classical canon must be considered and honored. Music publishers and distributors have capitalized on the need for multicultural music and profited from the sale of watered-down ethnic music for decades. A recent example is Sean O'Loughlin's *Imani* for concert band, published by Carl Fischer, LLC. The piece is marketed as a Kwanzaa piece for winter holiday concerts. The piece is described as having a "chant-like opening" (J. W. Pepper, 2022), where *chant-like* can be seen as a dog-whistle for *tribal* or *African*. The piece sounds similar to other concert band literature meant to depict the African continent, however, Kwanzaa is an African American celebration promoting empowerment within the Black community; and is not celebrated universally by African Americans. Kwanzaa was created in 1966 after the Watts Riots in California; Kwanzaa did not originate on the African continent.

Diversifying the music library and programming music by historically excluded composers can be seen as an expedient way of addressing racial and ethnic representation within music curricula via repertoire. Although diversifying repertoire is a step in the right direction, it is by no means the final destination, but rather a small part of the journey. Developing teacher competencies is essential for evaluating the classroom's music library. However, it is necessary to make choices that are informed by one's individual teaching circumstances, including community contexts and sociocultural contexts within the student population. Once repertoire is selected teaching must be appropriately scaffolded, in order to move toward authentic music learning and eventual performance.

Furthermore, it is necessary to research music and composers thoroughly. In 2019 composer Larry Clark was exposed for using the pen name "Keiko Yamada" posing as a Japanese woman, whose works depicted Japanese culture. In an interview with Jennifer Jolley, Clark explained the pen name was used in order to establish themselves as an orchestra composer because they were an established band composer (Jolley, 2019). However, members of online music teacher communities have alleged Clark's pen name was used to capitalize on calls for diversity in music education. Both rationales are sinister: the former connects to tropes and stereotypes about Asian people and orchestra, and the latter demonstrates a White male deceptively taking away space from people of color within the music education market.

Music Assessments, Competitions, and Adjudication

Musical assessments and competitions are a time-honored tradition in the music education field and are considered a regular activity in performance-based music classrooms (O'Leary, 2019). Though assessments and competitions are normalized, there are numerous barriers to equitable participation. Schools from urban and rural areas are typically not afforded the same resources as schools in suburban communities, though economically disadvantaged schools exist in all areas (Bates, 2012; Palmer, 2018). The expense of preparing and participating in assessments and competitions includes costs that are often passed on to families (e.g., private lessons/coaching, before and after school rehearsals, uniforms, transportation, food, lodging). Often success in assessments and competitions relies not on the quality of musical instruction, but on the enrichment opportunities and amount of resources available within a community (Bates, 2012; Palmer, 2018).

There is also rightful criticism over the content, reliability, and validity of adjudication criteria. According to Batey, "The very nature of assessment is subjective. Ratings are based on individual judgments. Adjudicators tend to grade more heavily on items they deem important" (2007, p. 73). Most often, these criteria are based on Western classical practice. Practitioner articles that offer advice to both teachers and adjudicators have demonstrated this bias. For example, Dumlavwalla (2018) encourages adjudicators to be familiar with standard repertoire, while Batey (2007) says a "neat and tidy appearance is foremost," yet further stating "most adjudicators will not grade down" if a group is untidy (p. 73). In this case *most* indicates that it is possible for adjudicators to grade down for circumstances beyond an ensembles' or students' control. Additionally, research has shown that adjudicators are likely to inflate or decrease grades based on non-musical factors like ensemble size, gender bias, instrumentation, and difficulty of adjudicated pieces (Antos, 2019; Rickels, 2011; Sullivan, 2003).

Participation in ensemble assessments and competitions disadvantages students from economically disadvantaged backgrounds. Furthermore, the reliance on ensemble assessments and competitions promotes passive engagement with diverse musics and marginalizes students' personal and cultural musical dispositions (Perkins, 2018). An anti-racist approach to music education disrupts the status quo by moving students and teachers away from the traditional teacher-centered teaching model found in music classrooms, moving toward student-centered and culture-centered learning; embracing a wide-range of diverse musics; expanding the scope of musical assessments; and developing culture-conscious students and teachers.

The Framework for Culturally Relevant and Responsive Music Teaching

Systemic change requires in-service music educators, music teacher educators, curriculum writers, instructional supervisors, and stakeholders to reflect on current practices that perpetuate social injustice and racist practices. Reflexivity is necessary to begin social justice and anti-racist work in music teaching and learning (Matthews, 2015; Palmer, 2018). In recent years, the field of culturally relevant pedagogy and culturally responsive teaching has emerged as a potential way forward for anti-racist education. The terms culturally relevant pedagogy and culturally responsive teaching are sometimes used interchangeably; however, we use both relevant and responsive because we believe that pedagogical choices should be relevant to students' lived experiences, encouraging both students and teachers to respond and take action. We use the term teaching because anti-racist teaching is ultimately the responsibility of teachers.

FCRRMT was developed from the vast body of literature associated with culturally relevant and responsive teaching. The framework takes into consideration the nuances of music teaching and learning, giving music teachers access points and pathways to using culturally relevant and responsive teaching effectively in their classrooms. The FCRRMT contains four quadrants: (a) teacher competencies, (b) informed choices, (c) authenticity, and (d) holistic/comparative lessons. It is anchored to Ladson-Billings' (1995) three tenets of culturally relevant pedagogy that include (a) academic achievement, (b) cultural competence, and (c) sociopolitical action. Ladson-Billings' (1995) work is rooted in Critical Race Theory (see Crenshaw, 1988) rather than multicultural education (see Banks, 2013). The connection to Ladson-Billings' (1995) culturally relevant pedagogy's three tenets, which center student empowerment, is woven throughout the four quadrants of FCRRMT (Palmer et al., 2022). The framework also connects to and encourages community engagement at all points in the teaching process; in every aspect of FCRRMT, community engagement is important to sustain connections to and bridge gaps between school and community. It is important for teachers to have an earnest commitment to enacting culturally relevant and responsive teaching, for when there is little understanding of the pedagogy, inconsistent implementation, or surface-level engagement, the pedagogy is unsuccessful and students do not foster deeper cultural connections or understandings, and academic achievement stalls (Dekaney & Robinson, 2014; Hynds et al., 2010; Sleeter, 2012). Using the framework with fidelity holds teacher and students accountable to fostering intercultural genuine relationships and engagement. FCRRMT supports the process of implementing and sustaining culturally relevant and responsive music teaching, and must be used to develop teaching practices within the teachers' specific teaching contexts.

Quadrant I – Teacher Competencies

The first quadrant, Teacher Competencies, contains five components: (a) developing cultural competence, (b) decentering Western art music and critical valuation of diverse musics, (c) community engagement, including culture bearers when appropriate, (d) open-disposition and checked personal and musical biases, and (e) facilitator role in

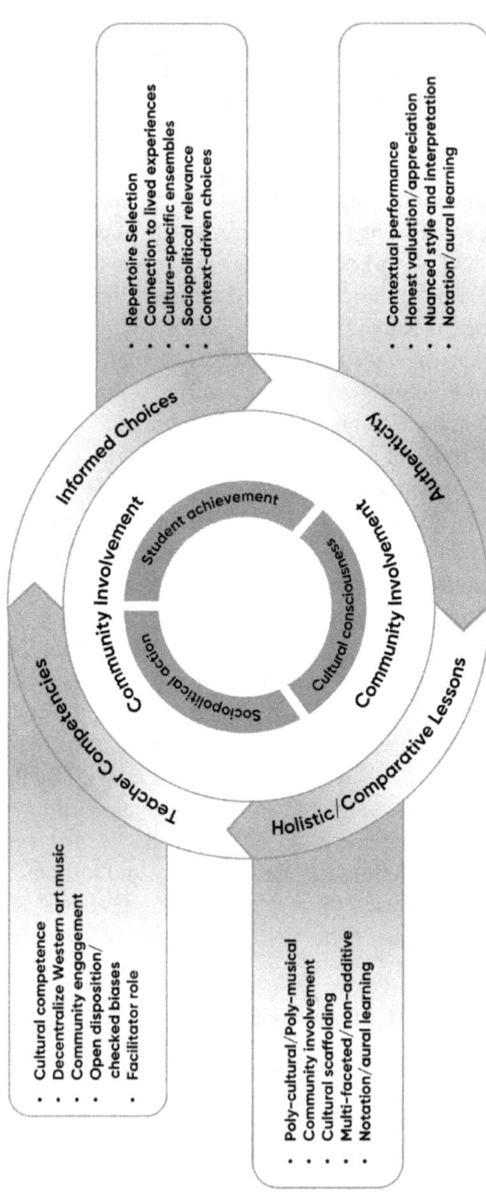

Figure 3.1 The Framework for Culturally Relevant and Responsive Music Teaching.

Source: Palmer et al. (2021).

nuanced conversations (Palmer et al., 2021). The personal development of core teacher competencies is a necessity for developing an empathetic understanding of cultures, identities, and music that are different from the teacher's point of reference (Palmer et al., 2021). As stated previously, undergraduate music programs largely teach through the White Racial Frame, where Eurocentric musical standards and tastes are upheld. The importance of decentering Western art music and considering the true value of music outside of Eurocentric aesthetics cannot be understated. Examining implicit and explicit personal and musical biases is required to view music beyond the White Racial Frame and Eurocentric aesthetics. Beyond examining personal implicit and explicit biases, the biases must be confronted and eradicated. A person with racial biases and White supremacist belief systems cannot fully engage in anti-racist work. Further, identifying and developing relationships with musical culture bearers is a step toward gaining appreciation and understanding of cultures and musical communities. Increased cultural competence and eliminating the White Racial Frame are essential for enacting culturally responsive pedagogy as a tool of anti-racism. Finally, the United States has complicated histories impacting present-day life, students from historically excluded backgrounds or with marginalized identities may be unable to leave their traumas outside of school. The ability to facilitate nuanced conversations is necessary for supporting students and student-centered and culture-centered instruction (Palmer et al., 2022; Shaw, 2016).

An example of developing teacher competencies is a critical examination of hip-hop culture and the nuances of hip-hop as music and other artistic expressions. A critical analysis of hip-hop culture reveals an evolution of music and fashion aesthetics, sociopolitical commentary and activism, alongside global popularity (Ladson-Billings, 2015). However, hip-hop, the culture and the art form, are often denigrated and dismissed. In 2018 rap artist Kendrick Lamar became the first rapper to win a Pulitzer Prize in music. A truly significant accomplishment was marred by backlash from members of the classical music community (Roberts, 2018). Increasing one's cultural competencies surrounding hip-hop's cultural norms and dispositions, alongside gaining applicable knowledge of hip-hop's musical aesthetics creates an understanding of hip-hop's duality and its popularity within the United States and the world (Ladson-Billings, 2015). Having this knowledge positions hip-hop as a critically important curricular choice in music classrooms versus using hip-hop to create an initial connection with students, which may be seen as pandering. Engaging students in nuanced conversations about these and other social and political issues surrounding hip-hop and engaging with hip-hop artists from the community are further ways of developing and demonstrating teacher competency.

Developing teacher competencies is essential for evaluating the classroom's music library. In recent years there have been calls to program music composed by composers from historically marginalized backgrounds. Diversifying the music library and programming music by historically excluded composers can be seen as an expedient way of addressing racial and ethnic representation within music curricula. However, it is necessary to make choices that are informed by one's individual teaching circumstances, including community contexts and sociocultural contexts within the student population. Once repertoire is selected teaching must be appropriately scaffolded, in order to move toward authentic music learning and eventual performance.

Quadrant II – Informed Choices

Quadrant two addresses the informed choices teachers make in designing music instruction that is socially just, anti-racist, and relevant and responsive to students' lives. Quadrant two includes (a) repertoire selection, (b) connection to lived experiences, (c) culture-specific ensemble formation, (d) sociopolitical relevance, and (e) context-driven choices (Palmer et al., 2021).

As teachers make choices about music instruction, they must bear in mind that what they do in the classroom is never done in isolation. The process of education occurs within multiple, overlapping layers of context. These layers include everything from the student's personal context of home, family, and friends, to the context of the global community that is ever-increasingly interconnected by commerce, technology, and cultural exchanges. When teachers make choices that align with global, local, and personal contexts, they connect teaching and learning with students' lives and with the sociopolitical forces that are constantly at work in the world, in nations and states, in local communities, and in schools themselves.

This contextual alignment is in keeping with Critical Pedagogy for Music Education as described by Abrahams (2017) who advocates learning that is relevant to the student's world. An example of this alignment is the Modern Musician's Project created by Jilian Burgam, a general music teacher in Dearborn, Michigan. In this project, students research a musician of their choosing, create a multimedia presentation, and present their findings to the class. Another example is Burgam's Musical Heritage Project in which students interview family members about their personal and/or ethnic musical heritages, fostering community within family contexts.

Personalization and contextualization can also be applied to repertoire selection in school music ensembles. Shaw (2012) wrote that it can be challenging to reflect the heritages of all students in ensemble repertoire, because school ensembles, by their nature, typically only learn and perform a limited number of pieces each year (although this need for "perfection" may itself be a symptom of Eurocentrism at work). Shaw suggests a spiral curriculum in which students study a limited number of musical cultures in depth over their three, four, or more years at an institution. This is an improvement on the multicultural approach that exposes students to as many cultures as possible, thus lessening the depth of musical study and exploration. However, Shaw's spiral approach still falls short of the *individual* personalization and contextualization required by culturally relevant and responsive teaching.

Work must also be done to make sure that repertoire selections can be appropriately taught in the school context, and that pieces are taught in a similar manner to which they are learned in their original contexts. Repertoire can also be checked for its applicability to students' lives, to the needs of the school and local community, and for its ability to create opportunities for dialogue. Finally, repertoire should be considered not only for its ability to develop students' skills, but for its relevance to students and culture. Students may even be engaged in making choices about what repertoire is studied (Abrahams et al., 2017).

The formation of culture-specific ensembles can also lead to a socially just, anti-racist music education. Examples of culture-specific ensembles include mariachi, gamelan, steel pan, folk music, and gospel ensembles. *A cappella*, hip-hop, rap, rock, and R&B ensembles are further examples that may connect with students' lived experiences. Culture-specific ensembles place culture and context in the forefront of the music-making experience and prioritize multiple forms of music teaching and learning. While these ensembles are sometimes added to existing school ensemble offerings like choir, band, and orchestra, they can also take the place of these "traditional" ensembles. Such experiences are enhanced when connected to community practice through shared musical experiences with school and community ensembles.

Shared experiences also help teachers connect what happens in the classroom with sociopolitical issues in the local community. While some teachers are encouraged to include social and politically relevant content in their classrooms, others are forbidden from (or afraid of) bringing "capital P" politics into the classroom. Sociopolitical issues do not have to do only with national politics. They can be any issue at the school, community, or even personal level that deals with societal issues and power structures. An example of this is the National Anthem Project created by suburban Philadelphia middle school music teacher Derek Cressman. Students first examine the United States' National Anthem, its history, and its musical characteristics. Students then work in groups to create a school or classroom anthem that exemplifies the values of the school community. Another example might be the exploration of what the terms love, justice, and peace mean for individual students, and how these themes are present in the music they study at school and listen to at home.

Quadrant III – Authenticity

Authenticity, the third quadrant of the framework, relates to the transmission and teaching of musical styles in all musical contexts. Authenticity supports music educators' experiences by addressing the "hows" of teaching. This quadrant includes (a) contextual performances, (b) honest valuation and appreciation, which includes appropriate knowledge of diverse styles of music and a nuanced understanding of style and interpretation, and (c) notational or aural learning. Authenticity requires teachers and students to engage with, explore, and immerse themselves in a variety of musical styles and to seamlessly move from style to style in performances representing the musical traditions of those in the classroom and community (Palmer et al., 2021).

In order to teach music authentically, teachers and students must together become learners and practitioners of diverse musical styles. This may be accomplished through immersive experiences with community music ensembles, or by bringing members of the community into the classroom as culture bearers. Technology including access to video conferencing software and video repository sites such as YouTube may assist teachers and students in these efforts. Understanding diverse musical styles from within enables students and teachers to value musical traditions on their own merits, rather than through comparison to Western classical ideals or through aesthetically based elements of music approach. Understanding music within its cultural context fosters honest valuation and understanding of music. While the classroom by its nature removes musical practice from its natural environment, contextualized performances can help students and audiences alike to understand music more authentically. Contextualized performances may take the form of "informances" where students teach each other and the audience about the works they are performing, or by siting school music performances in the community in side-by-side encounters with local musicians. These may also include performances that immerse musicians, audience, and community members where standard, Eurocentric Western notational styles may be unable to capture authentic nuances in music. Performances that provide cultural context for musical experiences can also help avoid cultural appropriation. Of importance is identifying ways in which to learn, plan, and facilitate musical experiences so that musical contexts are appreciated, not appropriated. Teaching authentically enables the emergence of genuine connections between music and students' lives. Authentic exploration and teaching begins with contextual knowledge of diverse musics beyond Eurocentric Western repertoire, followed by the cultivation of subtlety in musical style. Contexts and styles should extend beyond formal musical components such as dynamics, form structure, and articulation to cultural practices and meanings, such as the social and political phenomenon experienced by a composer or performance during a specific time and place, and should celebrate the diversity and subtlety of musical sound.

Honest valuation, or assessment, allows students and teachers to dive deep into the subtleties of the composition and performance process and immerse themselves within the nuances brought forth by the music. White Racial Framing and Eurocentrism preferences melody and harmony, often dismissing and denigrating music without melody. Honest valuation takes into account the musical elements present within a piece of music, rather than devaluing music based on which musical elements are absent. Furthermore, honest valuation makes space for understanding how diverse musics are discussed, performed, and experienced within their appropriate sociocultural and socio-musical contexts.

Understanding social and political context brings empathetic and honest connection to students and their lives. It is common for schools to celebrate cultural heritage months with student-lead cultural performances. Performances without social, historical, and musical context fall short of authentic interpretation, and risk cultural appropriation or being edutainment (Menkart, 1999; Palmer, 2018). During Black History Month (celebrated annually in the United States from February 1 to February 28) a school choir may sing *Follow the Drinking Gourd* (enslavement), *Lift Every Voice and Sing* (post-emancipation), or *We Shall Overcome* (Civil Rights Era). Each song has its own specific and unique context within the African American experience. Additionally, each song has been notated, but are often taught by rote, having various tempi, meter, and embellishments. Situating performances contextually through authentic means of transmission develops genuine understandings of culture, musical style, and social and contextual connections (Palmer et al., 2021). The connection fosters respect for cultural contexts and experiences. Without respect for cultural context performances may be viewed as cultural appropriation or worse, racist.

Authenticity can also refer to "what is real" (or authentic) for students in music classrooms. This can be developed through building relationships with each student in the *place* they are and from the perspective of *who* they are.

Considerations of authenticity in music teaching and learning can be found in studies by Elksund and Reistadbakk (2020) and Edwards (2022) as they invite music educators to consider authenticity from different perspectives of creativity, i.e., within topics of performance, storytelling, digital music making and music production, composition and songwriting. As we move to teach musical styles of multiple genres, we focus less on the White Eurocentric Western canon, we might use *Basics of Indian Classical Music with Anuja Kamat* (2014) to share the concept of different meanings for the word "classical." If we have string players in a general music class, we might offer the opportunity for a lesson plan including reading about, listening to, and discussion of the hip-hop string duo, *Black Violin*. As educators, we can apply educational understanding toward valuation of students' experiences from outside classrooms.

Employing authenticity most prominently considers interactions with students through the transmission and teaching of musical styles in all canons, but also from the perspective of what students are interested in learning about. Authentic teaching pedagogies can appear in music classrooms through not only listening to or performing, but also creating music. Original sound designs (digital technologies, often without text), compositions, or songs composed by students through independent or collaborative means can promote a range of positive characteristics while encouraging students to find their own authentic musical voice. Project ideas will most likely look different for each classroom, as all students bring uniqueness to the music room, even though project guidelines are the same. In other words, authenticity then emerges through unique extensions brought forth by the students to the foundational assignment. As well, projects may include opportunities for self-awareness, the nurturing of musical and social identities, student-centered thinking shared with other students, and critical reflection throughout the process of creating, sharing, and performing.

Quadrant IV – Holistic/Comparative Lessons

Designing holistic and/or comparative lessons requires consideration of five facets: (a) poly-cultural/poly-musical approach, (b) community involvement, (c) cultural scaffolding, (d) multi-faceted/non-additive elements, and (e) notation/aural learning (Palmer et al., 2021).

Making an intentional effort to give equal weight to the musics of diverse cultures, while explicitly not prioritizing Western classical art music over other music, moves the curriculum closer toward anti-racism and appreciating the music of various cultures. Bringing in culture bearers from the surrounding community deepens poly-cultural learning. Building mutually beneficial relationships over time can strengthen school and community bonds.

The teacher must take special care in designing carefully scaffolded lessons that will help all learners toward appreciation and cultural competence. With careful consideration, the teacher can design lessons that progress toward anti-racism. Without proper preparatory lessons that build toward deeper understandings of a given culture, students risk exoticizing a culture, and teachers risk falling into the act of tokenization. An example of tokenization in music classrooms is creating a gospel choir or performing gospel music without consideration to historical contexts to chattel slavery in the United States, religion as a pathway toward literacy for enslaved people, and gospel music's place in Africa's musical diaspora (Jones, 2018). Additionally, in selecting music to perform, it is important to consider the value of notational versus aural learning; for music of some cultures, aural learning may be a more appropriate and authentic practice than learning from written notation.

A holistic lesson and its overarching curriculum strive for a balance between mastering skills and understanding music as a cultural phenomenon. Learning to play a piece of music should also include learning about its performer, artist, or composer. The focus should not solely be on learning how to perform the piece, but also learning about the context that surrounds the piece. Students should be asked to consider the following questions:

- In what context did the artist write this work?
- Why did they write this piece?
- Was it a response to a cultural movement?
- Perhaps an expression of a personal issue the artist/composer was dealing with?
- What was going on historically at the time that the song or piece was composed?
- Was their piece written down, or improvised, or passed on orally?
- What was the historical and/or sociocultural context that gave meaning to this act?

Asking these kinds of questions moves the learning of music from a surface-level experience to a deeper, culture and justice-oriented, comprehensive learning experience. Holistic lessons consider local and global musical practices, helping students develop cultural competence. Students, community members, and the teacher are all part of the teaching and learning process, with the teacher as the facilitator who brings diverse perspectives and experiences into the classroom. Lastly, in holistic teaching, it is important to show how the song or piece is relevant to the students' lives.

An example of a holistic approach is exploring how music can be a response to social injustice, through performing and studying the protest song "I Can't Breathe" by artist H.E.R. (2020). In addition to learning the performance aspects and lyrics of the song, discussion about the context in which the song was written utilizes a multidisciplinary approach by discussing civics along the lines of historically marginalized people, police brutality, and systemic racism. Discussion of why the song was written combines emotion and expression with current events and challenges that society faces. Taking a step toward social justice means first understanding what social injustice is. Watching H.E.R.'s music video takes the lesson a step further, from the national to the international, as footage of protests worldwide makes clear that social injustice is a global concern. This lesson could be extended to looking at protest music in other countries. By making intentional musical choices and examining them for their cultural meanings beyond their formal qualities in a way that is relevant to today's learners, music teachers can disrupt the status quo and confront White supremacy. It is important to note, Quadrant IV may appear to be similar to world music pedagogy (Campbell & Scott-Kassner, 2014); however, FCRRMT "emphasizes student empowerment through sociopolitical context and dialogue as a part of [the] core pedagogy" (Palmer et al., 2022, p. 7).

Final Thoughts

PreK-12 and post-secondary music programs are not exempt from exclusionary practices and racialized aesthetics (Ewell, 2020). Feagin's White Racial Frame positions anti-racism as a counter-frame, opposing White supremacy. The counter-framing of White supremacy through anti-racist and socially just music practices are necessary to disentangle, undo, and/or thwart White supremacy at all stages of music teaching *and* learning.

Kendi's (2019) definition of anti-racism is supporting policies that lessen inequity and disenfranchisement of communities, where the inequity stems from race. Feagin (2020) writes, "antiracist counter-frames have provided important tool kits enabling individuals and groups to effectively counter recurring white hostility and discrimination" (p. 198). In PreK-12 and post-secondary music teaching and learning, the centering of Eurocentric aesthetics, musical thought, and musical intelligence is openly hostile toward music that does not fit within this frame. This is especially true in post-secondary learning (Ewell, 2020). Anti-racism in music teaching *and* learning requires a thorough examination of systems, policies, and curricular choices, and a radical disruption of institutions that disproportionately alienate and disenfranchise music outside of the Western art music canon.

FCRRMT provides a grounding for culturally relevant and responsive teaching that celebrates students' cultural identities and transforms the classroom into a place where real-world problems can be discussed and addressed through music. Using the FCRRMT creates pathways for musical aesthetics, musical intelligences, and musical thought that exist outside of the Western art music's White Racial Frame, to be discussed in earnest, as a whole entity, without depending on the canon of Eurocentric music. In this way the FCRRMT becomes a counter-frame within music teaching *and* learning at all levels.

FCRRMT moves the educational experience past product-driven teaching and learning, centering holistic knowledge acquisition, personal development and empowerment. Both teacher and students are engaged in growing their cultural competencies, addressing real-world problems, and increased engagement leading toward academic growth. Educators in PreK-12 and post-secondary music institutions must make social justice and anti-racist work the central focus of their guiding principles. Oppressive and hostile systems will not survive in the 21st century. As students begin to see themselves reflected in PreK-12 music classrooms, we may see more students of color and students with diverse musical backgrounds outside of band, orchestra, and choir find a place in undergraduate music programs. Using FCRRMT as a counter-frame interrogates topics that are included or excluded in music teaching and learning discourse, opening the profession to new possibilities for music creation, performance, and understanding. Music teachers and stakeholders can conceptualize music teaching and learning, where the learning environment is socially just and actively engaging in anti-racist work. Most importantly, the FCRRMT counter-framing radically reshapes how students experience their music education.

References

Abrahams, F. (2017). Critical pedagogy as choral pedagogy. In F. Abrahams & P. Head (Eds.), *The Oxford handbook of choral pedagogy*. Oxford University Press. https://doi.org/10.1093/oxfordhb/9780199373369.013.1

Abrahams, F., Rafaniello, A., Vodicka, J., Westawski, D., & Wilson, J. (2017). Going green: The application of Lucy Green's informal music learning strategies in high school choral ensembles. In F. Abrahams & P. D. Head (Eds.), *The Oxford handbook of choral pedagogy* (pp. 65–86). Oxford University Press.

Allsup, R. E. (2016). *Remixing the classroom: Towards an open philosophy of music education.* Indiana University Press.

Anderson, W. M. (1992). Multicultural music education: Introduction. *Music Educators Journal*, *78*(9), 25. https://doi.org/10.2307/3398425

Antos, J. (2019). An investigation into how contest outcomes affect student attitudes toward competitive marching band. *Journal of Band Research*, *55*(1), 18–48.

Banks, J. A. (2013). Approaches to multicultural curriculum reform. In J. A. Banks & C. A. McGee Banks (Eds.), *Multicultural education: Issues and perspectives* (8th ed., pp. 181–199). Wiley.

Bates, V. (2012). Social class and school music. *Music Educators Journal*, *98*(4), 33–37. https://doi.org/10.1177/0027432112442944

Batey, A. (2007). Preparing a high school choir for adjudication. *The Choral Journal*, *48*(6), 73–75. www.jstor.org/stable/23556799

Beyoncé. (Director). (2020). *Black Is King.* [Film]. Parkwood Entertainment.

Bonilla-Silva, E. (2015). The structure of racism in color-blind, "post-racial" America. *American Behavioral Scientist*, *59*(11), 1358–1376. https://doi.org/10.1177/0002764215586826

Brayboy, B. (2013). Tribal Critical Race Theory: An origin story of futures and directions. Theory in education. In M. Lynn & A. Dixson (Eds.), *Handbook of Critical Race Theory in Education* (pp. 88–100). Routledge. https://doi.org/10.4324/9780203155721

Campbell, P. S., & Scott-Kassner, C. (2014). *Music in childhood: From preschool through the elementary grades* (4th ed.). Schirmer/Cengage Learning.

Crenshaw, K. W. (1988). Race, reform, and retrenchment: Transformation and legitimation in antidiscrimination law. *Harvard Law Review*, *101*(7), 1331–1387.

Dekaney, E. M., & Robinson, N. R. (2014). A comparison of urban high school students' perception of music, culture, and identity. *Journal of Music Teacher Education*, *24*(1), 89–102. https://doi.org/dsnc

Dodd, J. (2020). *Being true to works of music*. Oxford University Press.

Dumlavwalla, D. (2018). Approaching the adjudicator's chair. *American Music Teachers*, *67*(5), 12–15.

Edwards, L. (2022). Dolly "5-9": Manufactured authenticity, transmedia storytelling, and Parton's star image. *Celebrity Studies*. https://doi.org/10.1080/19392397.2022.2116586

Elksund, J., & Reistadbakk, E. (2020). Knowledge for the future music teacher: Authentic learning spaces for teaching songwriting and production using music technology. In Ø. J. Eiksund, E. Angelo, & J. Knigge (Eds.), *Music technology in education – Channeling and challenging perspectives* (pp. 181–209). Cappelen Damm Akademisk. https://doi:10.23865/noasp.108.ch7

Elpus, K., & Abril, C. R. (2019). Who enrolls in high school music: A national profile of U.S. students, 2009–2013. *Journal of Research in Music Education*, *67*(3), 323–338. https://doi:10.1177/0022429419862837

Ewell, P. (2020). Music theory and the white racial frame. *Music Theory Online*, *26*(2), 1–29. https://doi:10.30535/mto.26.2.4

Feagin, J. R. (2020). *The white racial frame: Centuries of racial framing and counter-framing.* Routledge.

Freire, P. (1970/2000). *Pedagogy of the oppressed* (30th anniversary ed.). Continuum.

Gellerstein, B. A. (2021). *Daring to see: White supremacy and gatekeeping in music education. Graduate Doctoral Dissertations*. 647. University of Massachusetts, Boston. https://scholarworks.umb.edu/doctoral_dissertations/647

H.E.R. (2020). I can't breathe. YouTube. [Song]. Retrieved from www.youtube.com/watch?v=IRZWiqBHYaY

Hess, J. (2015). Decolonizing music education: Moving beyond tokenism. *International Journal of Music Education*, *33*(3), 336–247. https://doi.org/10.1177/0255761415581283

Hynds, A., Sleeter, C., Hindle, R., Savage, C., Penetito, W., & Meyer, L. H. (2010). Te Kotahitanga: A case study of a repositioning approach to teacher professional development for culturally responsive pedagogies. *Asia-Pacific Journal of Teacher Education*, *39*(4), 339–351. https://doi.org/bvkx3x

Jolley, J. (2019, November 7). The curious case of Keiko Yamada. *NewMusic USA*. https://newmusicusa.org/nmbx/the-curious-case-of-keiko-yamada/

Jones, D. A., (2018). Slave evangelicalism, shouting, and the beginning of African American writing. *Early American Literature*, *53*(1), 69–95. https://doi.org/10.1353/eal.2018.0003

J. W. Pepper (2022) *Imani by Sean O'Laughlin*. www.jwpepper.com/Imani/2465326.item#.YyAQw-zML8E

Kajikawa, L. (2019). The possessive investment in classical music: Confronting legacies of white supremacy in U.S. schools and departments of music. In K. Crenshaw (Ed.), *Seeing race again: Countering colorblindness across the disciplines* (pp. 155–174). University of California Press. https://doi.org/10.1525/9780520972148-008

Kamat, A. (2014). Introductory episode: Basic theory of Indian classical music. From web series: "*Basic Theory of Indian Music*."

Kendi, I. X. (2019). *How to be an antiracist*. Random House Publishing Group.

Ladson-Billings, G. (1995). Toward a theory of culturally relevant pedagogy. *American Educational Research Journal*, 32(3), 465–491. https://doi.org/10.3102/00028312032003465

Ladson-Billings, G. (2015). You gotta fight the power: The place of music in social justice education. In C. Benedict, P. K. Schmidt, G. Spruce, &P.

Woodford (Eds.), *The Oxford handbook of social justice in music education* (pp. 406–419). Oxford University Press.

Lind, V. R., & McKoy, C. L. (2016). *Culturally responsive teaching in music education: From understanding to application*. Routledge.

Mason, E. (2010). Multicultural music represented in current elementary music textbooks: A comparative study of two published music series. *Update: Application of Research in Music Education*, *28*(2), 29–41. https://doi:10.1177/8755123310361767

Matthews, R. (2015). Beyond toleration: Facing the other. In C. Benedict, P. K. Schmidt, G. Spruce, & P. Woodford (Eds.), *The Oxford handbook of social justice in music education* (pp. 238–249). Oxford University Press.

Menkart, D. J. (1999). Deepening the meaning of heritage months. *Educational Leadership*, *56*(7), 19–21.

Mineo, L. (2020, June 4). Orlando Patterson says there's been progress, but the nation needs to reject white supremacist ideology, bigotry in policing, and segregation. *The Harvard Gazette*. https://news.harvard.edu/gazette/story/2020/06/orlando-patterson-explains-why-america-cant-escape-its-racist-roots/

O'Flynn, J. (2005). Re-appraising ideas of musicality in intercultural contexts of music education. *International Journal of Music Education*, *23*, 191–203. https://doi.org/10.1177/0255761405058238

O'Leary, E. J. (2019). A phenomenological study of competition in high school bands. *Bulletin of the Council for Research in Music Education, Spring*, *220*, 43–61. https://doi.org/10.5406/bulcouresmusedu.220.0043

Palmer, E. S. (2017). *Forming relationships: Investigating social capital in a low socio-economic school music program* (Order No. 11016033). University of Southern California. Available from ProQuest Dissertations & Theses Global. (2158003603).

Palmer, E. S. (2018). Literature review of social justice in music education: Acknowledging privilege and oppression. *Update: Applications of Research in Music Education*, *36*(2), 22–31. https://doi.org/gft7tq

Palmer, E. S., Vodicka, J., Hyunh, T., D'Alexander, C., & Crawford, L. (2021). Grounded framework for culturally relevant and responsive music teaching. *Update: Applications of Research in Music Education*, *41*(1). 24–33. https://doi.org/10.1177/875512332110558

Palmer, E., Vodicka, J., Huynh, T., D'Alexander, C., & Crawford, L. (2022). Culturally responsive pedagogy. In F. Abrahams (Ed.), *A music pedagogy for our time* (pp. 41–60). GIA.

Perkins, J. D. (2018). What is written on our choral welcome mats? Moving beyond performative culture towards a more just society. *The Choral Journal*, *59*(5), 28–39. www.jstor.org/stable/26662695

Rabaka, R. (2013). W.E.B. Du Bois' contributions to critical race studies in education: Sociology of education, classical critical race theory, and proto-critical pedagogy. In M. Lynn & A. Dixson (Eds.), *Handbook of Critical Race Theory in Education* (pp. 69–87). Routledge. https://doi.org/10.4324/9780203155721

Rickels, D. A. (2011). *A multivariate analysis of nonperformance variables as predictors of marching band contest results* (Doctoral dissertation). Boise State University. Available from ProQuest Dissertations and Theses database. (UMI No. 3353883)

Roberts, R. (2018, April 11). Kendrick Lamar's Pulitzer Prize sparks lively – and at times snobby – conversations on the aesthetics of music. *Los Angeles Times.* www.latimes.com/entertainment/music/la-et-ms-kendrick-pulitzer-reactions-20180420-story.html

Shaw, J. (2012). The skin that we sing: Culturally responsive choral music education. *Music Educators Journal, 98*(4), 75–81. https://doi.org/10.1177/0027432112443561

Shaw, J. (2016). "The music I was meant to sing": Adolescent choral students' perceptions of culturally responsive pedagogy. *Journal of Research in Music Education, 64*(1), 45–70. https://doi.org/10.1177/0022429415627989

Sleeter, C. E. (2012). Confronting the marginalization of culturally responsive pedagogy. *Urban Education, 47*(3), 562–584 https://doi.org/10.1177/0042085911431472

Sullivan, T. M. (2003). *Factors influencing participation of Arizona high school marching bands in regional and state festivals* (Doctoral dissertation). Northern Arizona University. Available from ProQuest Dissertations and Theses database. (UMI No. 3080892).

Young, L. (2021). White supremacy: America's roots [Video]. TEDx Ohio State University. www.ted.com/talks/luther_young_white_supremacy_america_s_roots

4 Disrupting Ableism in Music Education through Preservice Preparation

Amanda R. Draper

"Who Are Our Exceptional Learners?"

This is a question I have often posed to undergraduate and graduate students in music education. Usually, the students will begin by making a list of diagnoses with which they are familiar; students with autism or Down syndrome, students who use wheelchairs, students with visual or hearing impairments. Sometimes they will include students with anxiety or ADHD, and occasionally they will consider students who are considered talented and gifted, students for whom English is not their first language, or a student with a temporary impairment such as a broken leg or a concussion. They rarely get to the end of this list without some prompting. I end the discussion around this question by pointing out that any student who is new to music would be an exceptional learner in an advanced music class. Through this process, the students eventually come to the realization that everyone learns and experiences the world in different ways. Despite this, beliefs and practices in music education tend to favor the typically-developing child, which is more of a myth than an actual student (Baglieri et al., 2011). In reality, students labeled with a disability or other exceptional learning style are often marginalized due to inaccessible classroom environments, one-size-fits-all curriculum, and instructional approaches that serve a select few musicians. It is these barriers that may be disabling to a student, not the students themselves.

Ableism is the belief that being non-disabled (i.e., "able-bodied" or "able-minded") is superior to having a disability or impairment (Baglieri & Lalvani, 2020). Similar to racism, classism, sexism, etc., it begins with a belief in the superiority of one population of people

DOI: 10.4324/9781003410645-4

and the inferiority of another, in this case contributing to the discrimination of people with disabilities. The ableist view that people with disabilities are not capable of participating or exceling in life activities is so common that it is regarded as a "permissible prejudice" that is implicit and considered acceptable in society (Baglieri & Lalvani, 2020).

Despite calls to counter ableism and better support students labeled with disabilities in music classrooms (Darrow, 2015), with a few notable exceptions (Hammel & Hourigan, 2017; Jellison, 2015), practitioner and research literature has typically addressed the music teaching and learning of students with disabilities as separate from music teaching and learning of students more broadly. If future music educators have an opportunity for preservice preparation with students with disabilities, it is most often through coursework outside of the school of music. I do not make these points to disparage these important contributions to the field, but to illustrate that the implicit message is that *music education for students with disabilities* is something different from *music education*, which I suggest perpetuates ableist views that serve to further marginalize this population.

To combat this, music teacher educators can look to the guiding tenets of Disability Studies in Education (DSE) that call us to promote equity and inclusivity with full and meaningful access to educational opportunities and to assume the competence of our students while rejecting deficit models of disability (Connor et al., 2008). Further, incorporating the Universal Design for Learning (UDL) model (CAST, 2018) into preservice music education course work could serve to disrupt the cycle of ableism and prepare future music teachers to identify the ways in which their practice and instructional environments may be disabling to students in their classrooms.

In this chapter, I briefly explore the idea of inclusive music education and draw on scholarship from disability studies (DS) to illustrate the need to disrupt the cycle of perpetuating ableism in music education. I propose the point at which this will be most impactful is within preservice preparation as there is the potential to influence the thinking of individual practitioners and impact their future music students as well. To do this, I will offer recommendations for including the UDL framework in preservice music education preparation courses. I suggest an approach that includes: (a) preservice teacher experiences with the framework as learners; (b) guided instruction in UDL and DS theory and philosophy; and (c) opportunities to design and execute UDL in practica with musicians of all abilities.

Who Is Music Education For?: Troubling Inclusive Music Education

Baglieri et al. (2011) challenged the notion of "inclusive education," which in theory should be open and "inclusive" of all learners. However, in most cases, "inclusive education" is the acceptable terminology for the inclusion of students labeled with a disability into what is understood to be the typical classroom. Rather than teaching and learning that is open and accessible for all learners, the education is "inclusive" as long as the student with disabilities is able to assimilate to the norms of the classroom. The responsibility is on the individual student to remediate a perceived deficit so that they may engage in these spaces in a "normal" way.

This individualized, deficit-based view is how disability (and disability in education) has historically been perceived; problematizing the person with an impairment (Connor et al., 2008; Oliver, 2009). For example, in a music education context, a musician who uses a wheelchair is not able to march and therefore may be excluded from the marching band in their school. Scholars in the field of DSE have proposed that theory, research, and educational practices must instead be guided by the perspective that disability is a social construct (Connor et al., 2008). The social model of disability places the problem with the societal response to individuals with impairments due to beliefs, expectations, and structures that favor a normative body (Oliver, 1990). Considering the music education example, was the musician excluded because of the societal expectations of what a marching band should look like? Did the musician self-select out because the environment and structures of the classroom were unwelcoming to a person using a wheelchair? By exploring our own beliefs and practices through this lens we may recognize ways in which we are unintentionally contributing to the disablement of our students.

Baglieri et al. (2011) theorized that (re)claiming the term inclusive education in a way that is genuinely accepting of all student variability requires deconstructing notions of "normalcy." Who is music education for? Is it meant only for those who can engage with it in typical ways? Is inclusive music education something different from music education in general? By critically examining the ableist structures and societal expectations surrounding these questions and inclusive music education, as well as interrogating our own actions and biases, we may come to recognize how we inadvertently construct boundaries limiting participation in music education to those who can operate within the "normal." It is not the burden of a student to change to fit the space, instead educators seeking truly inclusive music education should be open to expanding its boundaries to be accessible and accepting of all the ways in which students may be musical.

Disrupting the Cycle – Universal Design for Learning in Preservice Music Education

How do we as a field cultivate truly inclusive music education? I suggest we begin with future music educators by incorporating the UDL model in methods coursework and preservice preparation. This flexible pedagogical model holistically encompasses both teacher philosophy and praxis. In the following sections, I explain the principles of UDL and the habits of mind that contribute to practitioners' willingness and success with implementation. I then detail how the UDL model could be incorporated into preservice music education preparation. Fostering preservice music educators' understanding and motivation pertaining to UDL has the potential to not only influence the individual thinking of these future practitioners but also impact learning and the perceptions of ability among all their future music students.

Universal Design for Learning

The concept of universal design evolved within the field of architecture during the 1950s. Architects seeking ways to meet the legislative requirements that guaranteed access to public spaces for individuals living with disabilities recognized the benefits of barrier-free designs for all individuals (Center for Universal Design, 2008). The principles of universal design (see Table 4.1) guide the development of products and environments that ensure accessibility for all people, to the greatest extent possible, without adaptation. For example, a design that features a ramp as the main entrance to a building is useful for all individuals and does not create a barrier to entry for those who use

Table 4.1 Principles of Universal Design

1. Equitable use
2. Flexibility in use
3. Simple and intuitive use
4. Perceptible information
5. Tolerance for error
6. Low physical effort
7. Size and space for approach and use

Source: Center for Universal Design (1997).

wheelchairs, those with limited mobility, or persons pushing a cart or stroller.

Scholars and researchers with CAST (formerly known as the Center for Applied Special Technology) developed UDL by extending the principles of universal design to learning environments (CAST, 2021). Central to the philosophy behind UDL is an assumption that student variability is typical and the use of this framework encourages teachers to be proactive in designing environments, curriculum and instruction, and assessment to support their students' access, participation, and progress (Meyer et al., 2014). The UDL framework has three main principles: (a) providing multiple means of engagement; (b) providing multiple means of representation; and (c) providing multiple means of action and expression (Meyer et al., 2014). These are further delineated into guidelines and checkpoints that support the application of these principles in practice.

Multiple Means of Engagement

This principle focuses on the "why" of learning by helping students develop interest, purpose, motivation, and self-regulation (Meyer et al., 2014). A student's understanding of "why" they should be interested in a learning task will vary by student and task. Incorporating options to adjust demands and provide support will help learners to identify ways to connect with the learning experience, develop perseverance when challenged, and build on their own knowledge. Framework guidelines include providing options for developing the ability to self-regulate, options for sustaining effort and persistence, and options for recruiting student interest (Meyer et al., 2014). Following these guidelines may include facilitating student problem-solving when working on practice strategies, varying the requirements of an assignment or activity to ensure a motivating level of challenge, and offering students the opportunity to make authentic musical choices.

Multiple Means of Representation

Knowledge construction takes place when students perceive, interpret, and understand information within the environment. This principle addresses the "what" of learning by ensuring that the teaching methods and presented media and materials are not hindering students in the process of knowledge construction. This is done by providing options for comprehension, options for language and symbols, and options for perception (Meyer et al., 2014). Music educators may consider presenting materials in various formats, including making presentations, scores, recordings, and assignments available online in advance in addition to offering printed copies in class and sharing those materials aurally. Teachers should also consider students' prior knowledge, backgrounds, and understandings of language and musical symbols and how these factors may influence understanding of learning concepts.

Multiple Means of Action and Expression

The third principle addresses the "how" of learning by encouraging students to develop skills in planning and goal setting as well as offering various avenues for students to interact and express themselves as they construct knowledge. Supporting this is done by offering options for executive functions, options for expression and communication, and options for physical action (Meyer et al., 2014). In action, this principle may include teachers supporting students in short and long-term goal setting and encouraging the use of various forms of media and communication for demonstrating understanding and knowledge. Students may be given the choice of various options to demonstrate their understanding and skill development, such as writing a paper, creating a video, recording a podcast, or giving a presentation.

Cultivating Teacher Habits of Mind

In addition to the UDL framework for practice, the pedagogical model has evolved to include cultivating teacher habits of mind and philosophy that encourage the use of the principles (Meyer et al., 2014). Teacher habits of mind, such as a growth mindset toward learning, self-efficacy toward implementation, and self-regulation and motivation for teaching, are important components to teacher success with this model (Griful-Freixenet et al., 2021; Meyer et al., 2014). Meyer et al. (2014) emphasized that cultivating these habits of mind in combination with reflective practice are vital to developing teaching expertise.

Growth versus Fixed Mindset

Beliefs about the stability of ability exist on a spectrum between fixed and growth mindsets (Dweck, 2016). Teachers with a fixed mindset tend to view student traits such as intelligence or talent as predetermined. By contrast, a growth mindset is the belief that ability is malleable and can be developed through effort and guidance. Music educators may perceive musical talent as a fixed trait or as a skill to be developed with instruction and student effort. Teachers with a growth mindset are more likely to believe in their students' capabilities and utilize strategies like those within the UDL principles to support learning (Coubergs et al., 2017; Griful-Freixenet et al., 2021).

Teacher Self-Efficacy

Teacher self-efficacy is the belief that an individual has it in their ability to successfully guide student learning (Bandura, 1977; Woolfolk et al., 1990). Educators who are confident in their own capabilities tend to use more student-centered approaches (Woolfolk et al., 1990). A music educator with high teaching self-efficacy may use rehearsal strategies that focus on helping students identify errors in playing (e.g., asking guiding questions) rather than criticizing mistakes. A strong sense of self-efficacy is predictive of successful implementation of inclusive practices (Soodak et al., 1998) although it is context and task-specific (Bandura, 1977). Griful-Freixenet et al. (2021) found self-efficacy for implementing inclusive practices to be a strong predictor of preservice teachers' use of UDL.

Self-Regulation and Motivation for Teaching

In the context of UDL, self-regulation refers to teachers' ability to "identify, assess, reflect on, and revise their motivations" for teaching

(Meyer et al., 2014, p. 22). The self-determination theory (SDT; Ryan & Deci, 2000) details how behavioral regulation exists on a continuum from autonomous to controlled based on one's level of intrinsic and extrinsic motivation. The more a music educator feels personal value for teaching and experiences intrinsic motivation for the task, the more they feel in control of the experience (autonomous) and self-regulate their teaching. This leads teachers to adopt a teaching style that favors student autonomy (i.e., encouraging student choice; Pelletier et al., 2002). By contrast, music teachers who are motivated by external factors (e.g., money, rewards, opinions of colleagues, or the community) feel less personal connection to their teaching experiences (controlled regulation) and tend toward a more controlled teaching style that privileges their own perspectives over those of their students (Soenens et al., 2012). Teachers with a more autonomous regulatory teaching style encourage initiative and interest in their students and may be more apt to use UDL practices (Griful-Freixenet et al., 2021; Soenens et al., 2012).

Disability Studies in Music Education

Influencing preservice teachers' habits of mind and understandings regarding people with disabilities is critical to disrupting ingrained patterns of ableism and encouraging future use of UDL principles in practice. To guide this, I suggest we use the tenets of DSE which include:

- the contextualization of disability within social and political domains;
- privileging the knowledge, experiences, and voices of people identifying with a disability;
- promoting social justice, equity and inclusivity in educational opportunities, and full, meaningful access to society for people labeled with disability;
- and assuming competence and rejecting deficit models of disability (Connor et al., 2008, p. 448)

Music education coursework can include scholarship detailing the social model of disability and DS theory, as well as highlight practices that recognize disability as diversity. Course materials, guest scholars and artists, and musical works should include representation of musicians with disabilities. Implementing the UDL model should be framed as a way to support the variability of all learners, not just as a means to meet the needs of students with disabilities.

Importantly, music educators in higher education should demonstrate that they believe that musicians with disabilities are capable, and they should be advocates for social change that expands the notions of inclusive music education. To be sure, before the philosophy and habits of mind of future music educators can be influenced, music education faculty may need to confront their own beliefs with respect to people labeled with disabilities. Preservice music education is a potential point of disruption, but only with the guidance of faculty that recognize the need for change.

In a critique of disability discourse in education, Reardon and Ivey (2021) posed the questions:

> In what ways are teachers unconsciously ascribing students as dis/abled and altering their expectations to further construct their realities as being non-capable?… How can we move away from labeling students and toward seeing all students as having different and important needs?
>
> (p. 28)

I suggest we consider these questions within the context of personal, educational, and societal beliefs about musicians labeled with disability. In what ways do we assume the capabilities of a musician? How might our individual beliefs influence our expectations of our student musicians labeled with a disability? How do tokenized representations of musicians with disabilities and traditional notions of music education limit student opportunity, participation, and musical growth? Reardon and Ivey (2021) noted that the power to effect change lies with practitioners and those in preservice education. By engaging with DS theory and scholarship, future practitioners are exposed to views of disability that are counter to those traditionally held in education and well positioned to be the necessary agents of future change.

Universal Design for Learning in Music Methods: A Model for Incorporation

Preparing preservice teachers to use UDL in their future music classrooms requires development of teacher philosophy and habits of mind as well as experience with the framework for practice. Evans et al. (2010) described how one university explicitly integrated UDL principles in preservice preparation courses for special education teachers. The courses used a three-pronged approach of modeling, guided instruction, and student application of the framework in practice. To inform teacher philosophy and habits of mind, I propose that preservice educators also be given ample opportunity to engage with theory and scholarship from DS. The following sections will outline how I suggest this approach may be applied by music teacher educators to preservice methods courses.

Modeling in Higher Education

New educators should experience UDL as learners to develop a bank of experiences to draw from as teachers. Higher education classes tend to be lecture-based and dependent on visual and aural learning (Burgstahler, 2015). With a few small adjustments to preservice music education coursework, program faculty can model a more inclusive learning environment for these future teachers.

In the book *Teaching the postsecondary music student with disabilities*, McCord (2017) suggested strategies music faculty could use to include the principles of universal design in their courses. It is important to make the physical space of classrooms and rehearsal rooms as accommodating as possible for all learners and performers. Classroom arrangements, space allocation, entrances and exits, lighting, and clutter may negatively impact students and when possible, every attempt should be made to minimize these physical barriers.

Professors can examine their own classes through the lens of the UDL principles to optimize the accessibility of course content, activities, and instructional strategies to be welcoming for students with a variety of abilities. McCord suggested using backwards design, a component of Understanding by Design (Wiggins & McTighe, 2005), to ensure that assessment, instruction, and curriculum are accessible for developing understanding among all students. In backwards design, a course and its instruction are planned from the final goals backwards to ensure that all components are aligned to achieve the final outcomes (Wiggins & McTighe, 2005). Faculty can consider ways to explicitly include multiple means of engagement, representation, and action and expression during this backward design phase.

Immersing future educators in courses that are designed from the outset to be accessible for a variety of learning styles and abilities demonstrates a valuing of disability as a natural part of human diversity. This is an example of implicitly including the principles of DSE (Connor et al., 2008). Students in higher education are less likely to identify a personal need for disability accommodations either due to a lack of awareness of options at their institution or a desire to avoid the stigma of disability (McCord, 2017). An added benefit of the use of UDL in postsecondary education is that it ensures everyone has access to learning opportunities without the need for students to disclose a diagnosis. The inclusion of the principles of UDL in the planning and instruction of music methods courses provides students with a model of the framework and theory in action. Exposure to these elements within the context of learning about teaching the discipline weaves the experiences together and offers students a first-hand look at how UDL can be a part of teaching music.

Instruction in Universal Design for Learning and Disability Studies

CAST (2013) has a wealth of online materials that can support the initial introduction and theoretical grounding in the UDL framework. This should be supplemented with scholarship from within the discipline that provides examples of ways to utilize UDL in music education contexts (e.g., Armes et al., 2022; Darrow, 2016; Fuelberth & Todd, 2017; Fuelberth & Laird, 2014). In addition to modeling the framework within music methods courses, faculty can make use of guided instruction to draw attention to the principles of UDL within the context of instrumental, choral, and elementary methods courses. Guided instruction, drawn from constructivist approaches (Bruner, 1961), does not rely on direct lecture or "tell teaching" of a topic but instead challenges the learner to discover and construct the information themselves. Faculty guide this discovery-oriented process by facilitating discussions around the experiences with the modeled universal approaches to help the preservice music educators identify UDL in action and consider ways to apply it within their own teaching.

To promote this, methods courses could use an iterative process of modeling and guided instruction. The students are active participants in guided instruction as the course professor facilitates students' understanding of these principles in action. For example, in an instrumental methods course, faculty may model multiple means of representation as well as action and expression by demonstrating the proper hand positioning for an instrument (representation), by offering video links with the information for students who need to refer to it again at home (representation), and by giving students an opportunity to coach one another in pairs or small groups (representation/action and expression). When debriefing the process, the students are made explicitly aware of these principles in action. In the second iteration of this process, the professor teaches a class designed through the UDL lens and then leads a discussion about what the students may have noticed that made the lesson accessible for all learners. A further step may include having students discuss how they would represent the introductory learning process for their own instruments in multiple ways.

This cyclical approach of modeled experiences followed by guided instruction offers preservice teachers multiple opportunities to identify the principles in action and reflect on how they were applied. Throughout this process students should engage with scholarship from DS that challenges traditional notions of disability. This combination guides students in how to design learning environments that support student variability and to see why these practices are necessary and valuable.

Preservice Teacher Implementation

In the final step, preservice educators apply these experiences to their own budding teaching practices. This may be within the context of a class assignment or presentation, practicum, or student teaching experience. Students may use the UDL framework to analyze and assess if in-class presentations and peer teaching assignments are wholly accessible. Lesson plan assignments can include a component that encourages preservice teachers to demonstrate how they are certain all learners will benefit from the instruction. In-class options for implementation allows for this third step to become part of the iterative process of modeling and guided instruction. Importantly, it offers a space for real-time feedback on the integration of UDL.

Another significant time for preservice teachers to apply UDL is in practicum and student teaching experiences. The added benefit of these applications are interactions with actual students who will respond authentically to preservice teachers' activities. Field experiences are typically considered by practicing teachers to be one of the most valuable parts of teacher preparation (Bartolome, 2017; Conway, 2002, 2012; Groulx, 2016). These experiences are especially important in aiding teachers to feel prepared to work with students with disabilities (Bartolome, 2013, 2017; Hourigan, 2009). Preservice teachers may apply elements from the UDL framework to mini lessons taught during practicum experiences or on a larger scale within units taught while student teaching. The feedback that preservice teachers receive in these contexts comes directly from the students who are impacted positively or negatively by the experiences. Throughout these field experiences preservice teachers still receive the support of faculty, mentoring teachers, and peers to work through challenges that may arise in the implementation process.

Conclusion

Practitioner articles and books in music education have recommended the application of UDL in the K-12 music classroom (Adamek & Darrow, 2018; Darrow, 2010; Jellison, 2015) and universal approaches in higher education music (McCord, 2017). These practices are useful in supporting the learning needs of all students but disrupting ableism in music education will also require a shift in thinking. By offering experience and instruction in the UDL framework alongside examinations of DS theory, preservice educators are given tools to use in the classroom with opportunities to better understand the phenomenon of disability and develop ability-oriented habits of mind. This serves to cultivate a teaching disposition that focuses on student strengths and prepares preservice educators to design K-12 music education programs that truly welcome and support all learners. By redefining practice at the point of preservice preparation, future educators learn to teach to student ability rather than focus on *dis*ability, which may disrupt patterns of ableism and help to reframe inclusive music education as expansive for musicians of all abilities.

References

Adamek, M., & Darrow, A. A. (2018). *Music in special education* (3rd ed.). The American Music Therapy Association, Inc.

Armes, J. W., Harry, A. G., & Grimsby, R. (2022). Implementing universal design principles in music teaching. *Music Educators Journal*, *109*(1), 44–51. https://doi.org/10.1177/00274321221111486

Baglieri, S., Bejoian, L., Broderick, A., Connor, D., & Valle, J. (2011). [Re] claiming "inclusive education" toward cohesion in educational reform: Disability studies unravels the myth of the normal child. *Teachers College Record, 113*(10), 2122–2154.

Baglieri, S., & Lalvani, P. (2020). *Undoing ableism: Teaching about disability in K-12 classrooms*. Routledge.

Bandura, A. (1977). Self-efficacy: Toward a unifying theory of behavioral change. *Psychological Review, 84*(2), 191. https://doi.org/10.1037/0033-295X.84.2.191

Bartolome, S. J. (2013). Growing through service: Exploring the impact of a service-learning experience on preservice educators. *Journal of Music Teacher Education, 23*(1), 79–91. https://doi.org/10.1177/1057083712471951

Bartolome, S. J. (2017). Comparing field-teaching experiences: A longitudinal examination of preservice and first-year teacher perspectives. *Journal of Research in Music Education, 65*, 264–286. https://doi.org/10.1177/0022429417730043

Bruner, J. S. (1961). The act of discovery. *Harvard Educational Review, 31*, 21–32.

Burgstahler, S. E. (2015). *Universal design in higher education: From principles to practice* (2nd ed.). Harvard Education Press.

CAST. (2013). www.cast.org

CAST. (2018). *Universal design for learning guidelines*. National Center on Universal Design for Learning. http://udlguidelines.cast.org

CAST. (2021). *CAST timeline of innovation*. Center for Applied Special Technology. www.cast.org/impact/timeline-innovation

Center for Universal Design. (1997). *The principles of universal design, version 2.0*. North Carolina State University. https://projects.ncsu.edu/www/ncsu/design/sod5/cud/about_ud/docs/use_guidelines.pdf

Center for Universal Design. (2008). *About UD: Universal design history*. Retrieved August 29 from https://projects.ncsu.edu/ncsu/design/cud/about_ud/udhistory.htm

Connor, D. J., Gabel, S. L., Gallagher, D. J., & Morton, M. (2008). Disability studies and inclusive education—Implications for theory, research, and practice. *International Journal of Inclusive Education, 12*(5-6), 441–457. https://doi.org/10.1080/13603110802377482

Conway, C. M. (2002). Perceptions of beginning teachers, their mentors, and administrators regarding preservice music teacher preparation. *Journal of Research in Music Education, 50*, 20–36.

Conway, C. M. (2012). Ten years later: Teachers reflect on "perceptions of beginning teachers, their mentors, and administrator regarding preservice music teacher preparation". *Journal of Research in Music Education, 60*, 324–338.

Coubergs, C., Struyven, K., Vanthournout, G., & Engels, N. (2017). Measuring teachers' perceptions about differentiated instruction: The DI-Quest instrument and model. *Studies in Educational Evaluation, 53*, 41–54. https://doi.org/10.1016/j.stueduc.2017.02.004

Darrow, A.-A. (2010). Music education for all: Employing the principles of universal design to educational practice. *General Music Today, 24*(1), 43–45.

Darrow, A.-A. (2015). Ableism and social justice. In C. Benedict, P. Schmidt, G. Spruce & P. Woodford (Eds.), *The Oxford handbook of social justice in music education* (pp. 204–220). Oxford University Press.

Darrow, A.-A. (2016). Applying the principles of universal design for learning in general music. In C. R. Abril & B. M. Gault (Eds.), *Teaching General Music: Approaches, Issues, and Viewpoints*. Oxford University Press.

Dweck, C. S. (2016). *Mindset: The new psychology of success* (Updated ed.). Ballantine Books.

Evans, C., Williams, J. B., King, L., & Metcalf, D. (2010). Modeling, guided instruction, and application of UDL in a rural special education teacher preparation program. *Rural Special Education Quarterly, 29*(4), 41–48.

Fuelberth, R., & Todd, C. (2017). "I dream a world": Inclusivity in choral music education. *Music Educators Journal, 104*(2), 38–44.

Fuelberth, R. V., & Laird, L. E. (2014). *Tools and stories: Preparing music educators for successful inclusive classrooms through universal design for learning* 2013 VSA Intersections: Arts and Special Education, Washington D.C.

Griful-Freixenet, J., Struyven, K., & Vantieghem, W. (2021). Toward more inclusive education: An empirical test of the universal design for learning conceptual model among preservice teachers. *Journal of Teacher Education, 72*(3), 381–395. https://doi.org/10.1177/0022487120965525

Groulx, T. J. (2016). Perceptions of course value and issues of specialization in undergraduate music teacher education curricula. *Journal of Music Teacher Education, 25*(2), 13–24.

Hammel, A. M., & Hourigan, R. M. (2017). *Teaching music to students with special needs: A label-free approach* (2nd ed.). Oxford University Press.

Hourigan, R. M. (2009). Preservice music teachers' perceptions of fieldwork experiences in a special needs classroom. *Journal of Research in Music Education, 57*(2), 152–168.

Jellison, J. A. (2015). *Including everyone: Creating music classrooms where all children learn*. Oxford University Press.

McCord, K. A. (2017). *Teaching the postsecondary music student with disabilities*. Oxford University Press.

Meyer, A., Rose, D. H., & Gordon, D. (2014). *Universal design for learning: Theory and practice*. CAST Professional Publishing.

Oliver, M. (1990). *Politics of disablement.* Macmillan International Higher Education.

Oliver, M. (2009). *Understanding disability: From theory to practice* (2nd ed.). Palgrave Macmillan.

Pelletier, L. G., Séguin-Lévesque, C., & Legault, L. (2002). Pressure from above and pressure from below as determinants of teachers' motivation and teaching behaviors. *Journal of educational psychology, 94*(1), 186–196. https://doi.org/10.1037//0022-0663.94.1.186

Reardon, K., & Ivey, A. (2021). Problematizing the binary: A poststructural understanding of dis/ability in schools. In J. N. Lester (Ed.), *Discursive psychology and disability* (pp. 21–45). Springer.

Ryan, R. M., & Deci, E. L. (2000). Self-determination theory and the facilitation of intrinsic motivation, social development, and well-being. *American Psychologist, 55*(1), 68–78. https://doi.org/10.1037/0003-066X.55.1.68

Soenens, B., Sierens, E., Vansteenkiste, M., Dochy, F., & Goossens, L. (2012). Psychologically controlling teaching: Examining outcomes, antecedents, and mediators. *Journal of educational psychology, 104*(1), 108.

Soodak, L. C., Podell, D. M., & Lehman, L. R. (1998). Teacher, student, and school attributes as predictors of teachers' responses to inclusion. *The Journal of Special Education, 31*(4), 480–497. https://doi.org/10.1177/002246699803100405

Wiggins, G., & McTighe, J. (2005). *Understanding by design professional development workbook.* ASCD.

Woolfolk, A. E., Rosoff, B., & Hoy, W. K. (1990). Teachers' sense of efficacy and their beliefs about managing students. *Teaching and Teacher Education, 6*(2), 137–148. https://doi.org/10.1016/0742-051X(90)90031-Y

5 Administrator Approaches to Hiring for Music Positions

Jocelyn A. Stevens and Jill Wilson

Introduction

Calls to expand public secondary school music curricular offerings to include courses other than band, orchestra, or choir are hardly a new phenomenon (Freer, 2011; Jones, 2008; Leonhard, 1991). Indeed, very little has changed with respect to public school music over the last 100 years despite an increasingly interconnected global society, expansion of electronic performance and production, and the prevalent dissemination of music through digital media. As the College Music Society Manifesto authors reminded us, "The world into which our students will graduate is vastly different from the one around which the field has typically been conceived" (Sarath, 2017, p. 54).

Beginning in the 2000s, broader certification (often K-12 or PreK-12 music) was embraced to accommodate curricular demands (Greher & Tobin, 2006; Henry, 2005; May et al., 2017). For example, Schmidt et al. (2006) investigated public school music curricula in Indiana and determined that about 64% of the teacher participants had some sort of general music as part of their load. While it was more common for band directors to teach only band (59.8%), only about 35% of choral directors solely taught choral music, and the proportion of string teachers who focused exclusively on their specialty was 25.5%. Music teacher education programs, therefore, are charged with preparing future music educators to be able to reach students at all grade levels and who have varied needs and goals.

While much research is dedicated to the role of the university in preparing future music educators to enact curricular change (Colley, 2009; Essex, 2010; Groulx, 2016; Hickey & Rees, 2002; Hourigan & Scheib, 2009; Kimpton, 2005; Mantie et al., 2017; Sarath et al., 2017;

DOI: 10.4324/9781003410645-5

Teachout, 2005; Thornton et al., 2004; Williams, 2007; Younker & Hickey, 2007), few have connected these calls for change with the realities of the positions in which teachers are employed (Abril & Gault, 2008; Give a Note Foundation, 2017; Groulx, 2016; Prendergast, 2021; Schmidt et al., 2006). Many music educators teach outside their area of specialization at some point in their career (Groulx, 2016) and secondary level educators often teach music classes that are not band, choir, or orchestra (non-BCO) (Prendergast, 2021; Schmidt et al., 2006). This demonstrates a need for broader preparation of preservice teachers, which aligns with what Conway (2012) determined was a recommendation from experienced music educators.

Expanding the secondary school curriculum is complicated by many factors, not least of which is the reifying large ensemble tradition at the secondary level, which is further bolstered by preservice teacher curricula. Intentional disruption may be necessary to bring about change to make music programs relevant and inclusive in the 21st century (Williams, 2019), thereby reaching the "other 80%" (Culp & Clauhs, 2020) or the majority of high school students nationwide who choose not to participate in school music (Elpus & Abril, 2011; Elpus & Abril, 2019; Williams, 2007). One possible place for disruption that has not been explored is at the public school administrator level. While some principals have indicated a desire to expand secondary school music offerings to include other classes, such as piano, guitar, music technology, and/or rock band (Abril & Gault, 2008; Byo, 2018) these desires may not be widespread or may be complicated by unknown factors. Understanding what administrators look for in candidates when hiring for open music positions and what they value in their school music programs is an important part of understanding, and possibly disrupting, this reifying structure of secondary music education in the United States.

Review of Literature

According to Engel and Curran (2016), organizational management skills, which include the hiring of new teachers, play a key role in principal leadership and responsibility. The hiring of new teachers may have the greatest effect on student outcomes (Engel & Curran, 2016). Many researchers acknowledge that hiring is the single most important task an administrator undertakes (Bolz, 2009; Hughes, 2014; Mason & Schroeder, 2010; Peterson, 2002) and a poor decision can cause problems and a decline in programs and school culture for multiple years

(Mason and Schroeder, 2010). Given the importance of the hiring process, there is a surprising lack of literature examining how administrators approach their hiring practices in general and the authors could identify no research examining this topic in the field of music education.

Current Programs

Several researchers have investigated music course offerings at the state level (Kelly & Veronee, 2019; Prendergast, 2021; Sanderson, 2014; Schmidt et al., 2006). Schmidt et al. (2006) investigated the music curricula in Indiana and found that general music was the most common offering, followed by choral music and band. The researchers further determined that between 40% and 75% of teachers who responded to the survey also taught some kind of general music. Similarly, Prendergast (2021) sought to determine the music course offerings in Iowa, Illinois, and Missouri, and BCO and elementary/general music were the most common. She also determined that, of those teaching at the secondary level, over a quarter of Iowa teachers, over a third of Illinois teachers, and almost half of the Missouri teachers taught a non-BCO class.

Sanderson (2014) sought to determine what made up the non-BCO offerings in the state of Nebraska. Almost three quarters reported having such an offering, largely consisting of music theory and music appreciation. Guitar class was the next most common course, followed by music technology and music history. Similarly, Kelly and Veronee (2019) examined existing courses offered at the schools through a survey of music students who were attending a large university-based summer camp in the southeastern United States. They were interested to learn about high school students' thoughts regarding "non-traditional" music classes. The five most common non-BCO offerings found in the programs were advanced placement (AP) music theory, musical theater, piano/keyboard class, music theory, and guitar ensemble. When asked in which they would be excited to enroll, music composition and arranging, AP music theory, music theory, music history, and piano/keyboard were commonly selected. Juchniewicz (2007) determined that, when selecting from a provided list of 21 "non-traditional" music classes, members of the Florida Bandmasters Association who responded to the survey indicated they would like to teach music theory as well as jazz ensemble and percussion ensemble, which indicates that some students and music educators have desires to take/teach non-BCO courses.

While large ensemble performance classes offered at the secondary level might seem ubiquitous, Elpus and Abril (2011) determined that, in 2004, only 21% of seniors nationwide were participating in BCO. The authors undertook a similar study almost a decade later to examine the demographic make-up of high school music programs (Elpus & Abril, 2019) and changes were minimal; 24% had participated in ensembles for at least one year. Indeed, substantial numbers of students drop out of large ensemble programs each year (as described in Byo, 2018; Hash, 2021; Williams, 2007). They remain ever present, regardless of the lack of a national standardized curriculum mandating that large ensembles serve as the core of secondary school music offerings, suggesting that they are of value to at least some stakeholders, even if it is not entirely clear who is primarily responsible for the decision to offer large ensembles in so many schools.

Importance of Dispositions, Skills, and Pedagogical Knowledge

In addition to the development of musical and pedagogical skills, researchers have shown that personal, or dispositional, factors contribute significantly to the effectiveness of teachers (Button, 2010; Hamann et al., 1998; Teachout, 1997; Wayman, 2006). According to the Interstate Teacher Assessment and Support Consortium (InTASC, 2013), dispositions are "habits of professional action and moral commitments that underlie the performances play a key role in how teachers do, in fact, act in practice" (p. 6). Researchers have compared student teachers' and experienced music teachers' perceptions of teaching behaviors and skills (Madsen et al., 1992; Teachout, 1997) as well as perceptions of music teacher educators (Doerksen & Richter, 2007, 2009) and music faculty (Royston & Springer, 2015) and determined that dispositional skills may be as important or more important that musical or pedagogical skills. The same was true for music teacher educators (Doerksen & Richter, 2007, 2009; Wilson & McGinnis, 2018). Several researchers (Miksza et al., 2010; Rohwer & Henry, 2004; Royston & Wilson, 2022; Teachout, 1997) have found that both preservice and in-service teachers rank personal characteristics and teaching skill as more important than musical skill; in-service music teachers and music education majors rank professional dispositions as most important.

Teaching skills and personal traits are often also more important to principals than subject matter knowledge (Harris et al., 2010; Kono,

2010). In an examination of how principals screen applicants and what they look for in their teacher candidates, Mason and Schroeder (2010) determined that professional attributes are likely used in the initial screening of candidates and personal attributes come into play later in the face-to-face interview phase. Administrators tended to rely on the review of submitted documents and interviews and, far more rarely, teaching observations. Professional attributes like grades, reference letters, and documented experience are easier to measure than personal attributes like communication skills, enthusiasm, and work ethic. Personal attributes like excitement, appearance, confidence, and love of children were all rated higher than content or pedagogical knowledge. Ratings were similar regardless of school demographics, grade level, or size (Mason & Schroeder, 2010).

Administrator Desires

The decision about whether or not there will be a music position at a school is often made by the state and/or district school board (Abril and Gault, 2008) and the decision to provide funding for a position and the official offer to hire is usually made by district-level administration or school boards. However, it is the building-level administration that is often responsible for interviewing (Mason & Schroeder, 2010) and they have a large amount of autonomy over hiring decisions (Liu & Johnson, 2006). Further, administrators have a tendency to value personal characteristics more than content knowledge, especially when candidates are in the interviewing phase (Engel, 2013; Mason & Schroeder, 2010; Strauss, 1999), so administrator desires about what music courses are offered in their buildings may not be a prominent consideration in the hiring process. While not representing a large body of research, some scholars have examined what administrators value in their music programs. Abril and Gault (2008) determined that 98% of the 541 secondary school principals who participated in their study reported offering music in their school. While for 67% of those schools the decision to offer music was a state and/or district requirement, in 33% of the schools it was a building-level decision, suggesting that music classes are valued by some administrators regardless of whether or not they are mandated. While band and choir were by far the most common secondary school music offerings reported, almost a quarter of the principals from the Abril and Gault (2008) study indicated a desire to offer piano (22%), guitar (21%), and music technology (19%). The authors suggested interest in these course offerings might indicate that administrators value music education and want to include more students in school music.

Beyond valuing music generally, a recent case study (Byo, 2018) of a principal's personal taste for rock music in particular led to them employing a teacher who was an accomplished performer of vernacular music rather than one with a teaching license. The administrator reported appreciating the teachers' "enthusiasm, "withitness," and "consummate musicianship" (p. 25). The author cited the value of music, community, and identity that arose as a result of having a modern band program and suggested these are similar to those gained from traditional large ensemble participation. Administrators' desire for a music teacher with the ability to facilitate a sense of community and aid in the development of students' identity may be more widespread as they are, in large part, responsible for creating the environment Byo (2018) cited as being crucial to students' will to commit to and take ownership of their participation.

Summary

Large ensembles are the most common secondary level music course offerings despite the fact that the majority of students drop out of these ensembles. Some administrators have indicated a desire to offer non-BCO courses at their schools. Many music teachers are already teaching non-BCO classes, but it is not clear to what degree administrators value these music classes compared to others. While content knowledge and pedagogical skills are important and necessary for certification, personal dispositions are deemed more important by preservice and in-service teachers. This is also true for principals, who often have a large amount of autonomy in hiring decisions.

The purpose of this multi-phase study was to better understand the music positions for which administrators are hiring, as well as how administrators approach their hiring practices and what they value with respect to filling secondary level music positions. Therefore, we were guided by the following questions:

- What is the content of the advertised secondary school music teaching position openings?
- How do administrators approach the interview process when hiring for music positions?

- What personal, professional, and content-specific qualities do administrators value when hiring for music positions?

Method

This exploratory sequential mixed methods study (Creswell, 2014) began with a content analysis of secondary-level job postings in the Midwest (Phase I). Phase II, consisting of a multiple case study to examine administrator hiring practices for secondary school music teacher positions, followed. We then used results from Phase I and Phase II to inform the creation of a questionnaire that was distributed to a nationwide sample of secondary school administrators for Phase III.

Phase I

We undertook a content analysis of all music educator job openings in five Midwestern states (Illinois, Iowa, Kansas, Minnesota, and Missouri) during the months of April and May 2020. Data were collected from popular online job boards in each state and coded for size of community (using the NCES locale framework, which includes city – inside an urbanized area and inside a principal city, suburb – inside an urbanized area and outside a principal city, town – inside an urbanized cluster and outside an urbanized area, and rural – outside of an urbanized cluster and outside of an urbanized area), grade level(s), type of school (public, private, or charter), and any details about the job responsibilities (BCO, secondary general music, etc.).

Phase II

In order to explore how principals approach hiring music educators, the researchers employed a multiple case study design (Yin, 2018). We wondered what kinds of questions they ask during interviews and who they consult when hiring for music positions, as well as what personal, professional, and content-specific qualities they look for in candidates. We also wondered whether their aspirations for their music program inform their hiring practices. Interviews were chosen as they readily allow for the making of meaning through language and focus on individual views (Seidman, 2019). In the initial interview, administrators were asked to describe the current music offerings in their building as well as number of staff and how many of those staff they had been involved in hiring. We then asked what each looked for in a successful candidate and provided a list of content-specific skills and knowledge (ability to conduct, play piano, improvise, use technology, teach a variety of genres, etc.), asking the principals to rate the importance of each. Finally, we asked about their vision for the program and what roadblocks might prevent curricular change.

A second interview was arranged with each participant in order to ask follow-up questions about who creates job posting language in their district, whether they utilized music-specific interview questions, and who else, if anyone, they consult when hiring music positions. We also asked about their beliefs regarding the significance of charisma for non-music teachers, the relative importance of skills versus pedagogical knowledge, and the level of need for broad versus specialized training. Finally, we inquired about their vision for the future of their music program. Using a grounded theory (Corbin & Strauss, 2015) approach to analyze our interview data, we first assigned codes within cases then considered cross-case themes. We then engaged in member checking to improve the validity of our findings.

Phase III

Phase II provided preliminary understanding of how administrators approach their hiring for music positions and informed the creation of a large-scale survey for Phase III. We employed a questionnaire with three sections, informed by the work of Kersten (2008) and the findings from Phase II, to determine (a) demographic information, including the level for which they are administrators, how many music teachers are in their building(s), and how many music educators they have hired; (b) the various skills and dispositions they look for in a music teacher candidate; and (c) their school music program curriculum and desires for the future. The questionnaire was reviewed for face validity by the Phase II administrators and then the email addresses from selected states that were made publicly available on the Department of Education websites were collected. Using the six National Association for Music Education's Divisions as a guide, the questionnaire was sent to administrators from Georgia and North Carolina (Southern Division), Iowa and Minnesota (North Central Division), Nevada (Western Division), New Jersey and Rhode Island (Eastern Division), New Mexico (Southwestern Division), and Washington (Northwest Division).

Results

Phase I

Based on surveys, 80% of the openings described full-time jobs; 20% were part-time jobs. General music positions (or jobs that included some general music) represented 32.4% of the openings, while 61.1% did not include general music, and 6.5% were unclear descriptions. Pearson χ^2 tests of independence were used in order to determine significant relationships between the demographic data. Cramer's *V* was used to determine effect size and adjusted standardized residuals (ASRs) were used to interpret the significant results. (ASRs provide a way to measure the strength of the difference between the observed and expected values, with those greater than 1.96 indicated significance at $p < .05$ and those greater than 3.30 are significant at $p < .03$.) No significant relationship was observed between the size of community, $\chi^2(4, n = 185) = 6.49$, $p = .166$ or state, $\chi^2(4, n = 185) = 2.69$, $p = .612$ and advertising a position that explicitly included a secondary general music course.

A significant relationship was observed between the size of community and the grade levels of job, $\chi^2(20, n = 185) = 120.36$, $p < .001$, Cramér's $V = .40$, with rural districts being much more likely to advertise a PreK-12 position (ASR = 7.4) and districts in towns and suburbs being less likely (ASR = −2.5 and −4.3, respectively). Suburban school districts were more likely to advertise high school only positions (ASR = 4.1) and less likely to advertise for combined middle school/high school positions (ASR = −2.2). Finally, school districts in towns were more likely (ASR = 2.8) and rural districts were less likely (ASR = −3.3) to advertise for unspecified music openings.

Finally, a significant relationship was observed between the size of community and the type of job advertised, $\chi^2(20, n = 185) = 73.50$, $p < .001$, Cramér's $V = .32$. School districts in towns were more likely to advertise band positions (ASR = 2.9), while rural school districts were much more likely to advertise combined vocal and instrumental positions (ASR = 5.5). Both towns and suburbs were less likely to advertise combined vocal and instrumental positions (−2.5 and −3.4, respectively). School districts in cities were more likely to advertise for unspecified music positions (ASR = 3.4). Finally, suburban school districts were more likely to advertise for an orchestra position while rural school districts were less likely (ASR = −2.7).

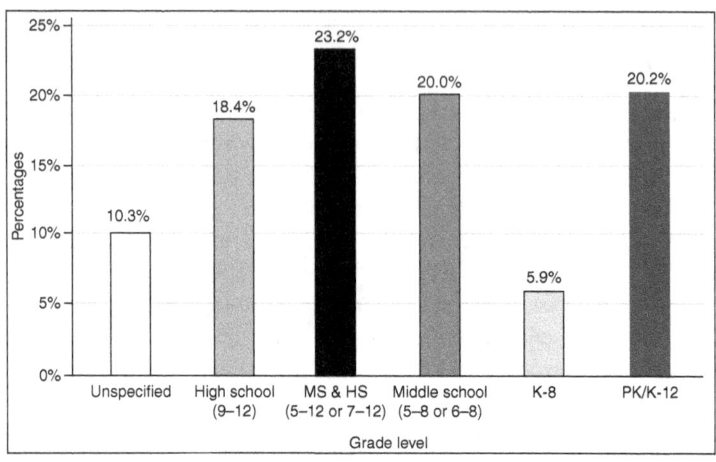

Figure 5.1 Percentage of Openings by Grade Level of Job.

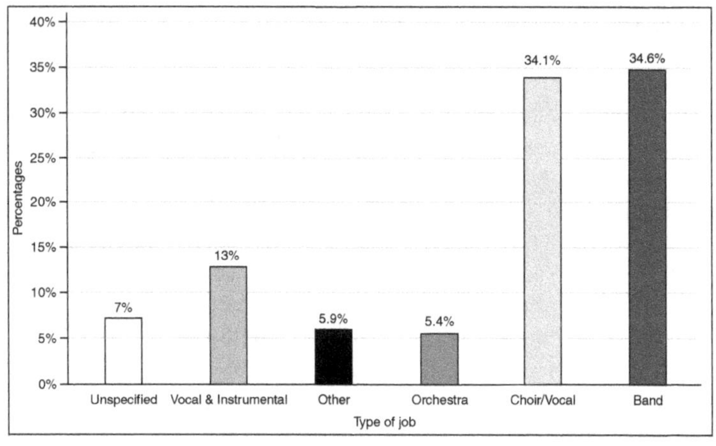

Figure 5.2 Percentage of Jobs by Type of Job.

Phase II

Three principals were interviewed in Phase II of the study. Principal I was a veteran administrator at a rural high school that offers band, choir, music appreciation, and two levels of class guitar. He reported approximately 200, or 50% of the school students in the building, were enrolled in a music class. In the last five years he had hired five music teachers. Principal II, a new administrator with two years of experience in a town, reported that about 25% of his high school population of 767 students is enrolled in a music class at a school that offers band, choir, and guitar classes. In the last five years he had not hired any music teachers. Principal III was a veteran administrator at a large suburban school that offered BCO, guitar classes, and AP music theory. In this building, about 30% of his 2342 students were enrolled in a music class. In the last five years he had hired two music teachers.

After assigning codes within cases, four cross-case themes emerged. These included the need for a music educator to possess charisma, a preference for their hire to be flexible in terms of being able to teach a variety of classes, and aspirations for having the program reach as many students as possible. Finally, these administrators expressed a desire to have strong large ensembles.

Theme 1: Charisma

Charisma, or similar personality characteristics, was recognized as a helpful trait for a music educator to possess. Administrators used the terms "high energy" and "magnetism" as being useful for the community-facing aspects of the job, such as speaking at concerts or performing in the community, and also for the day-to-day aspects of the position, such as classroom management. Charisma is also important in order to grow a music program as students respond positively and want to be a part of something when the teacher is excited about what they're doing and communicates that excitement to others.

Theme 2: Flexibility

Principals valued music educators who are capable of teaching a variety of classes. One mentioned newly formed guitar classes and adaptive music classes that had just started at their school. Another believed students at their school had an interest in a composing class or a "second-chance" band (for high schoolers who would be beginners on their instruments). Teaching assignments can vary and having educators capable of teaching more than a single music specialty is useful for scheduling purposes.

Theme 3: Program Reach

Having as many students enrolled in a music program as possible was important to administrators. One specifically stated, "We want numbers." This is due to the value many administrators see a music education provides to students, as well as for the pride it can engender in a community. "Performance is a big one. We want to be successful. It's not as competitive as a sport, but in reality, it kind of is. So that's the big thing." One also shared a desire to include students who might not choose band, orchestra, or choir: "[Guitar has] made a difference. It brings music to kids who wouldn't necessarily pick up the trumpet or trombone."

Theme 4: Large Ensemble Desire

Principals shared a desire to include large ensemble offerings in their music programs. Various factors played a role, including student interest, link to community, and, in some cases, a default assumption that this is what a music program should include. While other music offerings are also desirable, these three administrators believe large ensembles to be non-negotiable requirements.

Phase III

A nationwide sample of secondary administrators served as participants in this phase. They completed a questionnaire with three sections: demographics regarding their experience with hiring music educators, what they look for in a music teacher candidate, and their school music program curriculum and desires for the future.

Demographic Information

Of the 93 respondents, 39.8% were high school principals, 36.6% were middle school principals, 12.9% were combined middle school/ high school principals, and the remaining were principals of some other combination of elementary, middle school, and/or high school. Almost half (47.3%) of the administrators who responded to the survey were from Minnesota and another 18.3% were from North Carolina. Thirteen (14%) were from Nevada, 8.6% were from New Jersey, 6.5% were from Georgia, two each from Rhode Island and New Mexico, and one from Iowa. Only 10.8% of the administrators were from city schools, 17.2% were from suburban schools, 36.6% were from town schools, and 35.5% were from rural schools.

While 20.4% of the respondents had not hired any music teachers in the previous five years, 74.5% had hired anywhere between one and five music teachers. Just over half (53.8%) of the administrators who responded to the survey have two music teachers in their building(s). Another 35.5% had either one music teacher (18.3%) or three music teachers (17.2%) and the remaining principals had four or more music teachers in their building(s). Administrators who had not hired a music teacher in the previous five years were asked to respond to questionnaire items according to how they would intend to hire a music educator.

Interviewing Practices

When asked about the interview questions they typically ask in music teacher interviews, 41.9% of the principals who responded to the survey indicated that they use mostly the same questions they would use for non-music teachers. Another 37.6% indicated that they split the interview question topics roughly evenly between music-specific questions and those that are not content-specific. No principals indicated that they asked *only* music-specific interview questions but 18.3% indicated that they asked *mostly* music-specific questions. Only two principals (2.2%) indicated that they ask no music-specific questions in interviews for music positions.

The overwhelming majority of administrators who responded to the survey (81.7%) indicated that a music teacher is part of the interview team when hiring a music teacher. Rarely is the music teacher given the primary responsibility for conducting the interview with the administrator simply signing off on the selected candidate (2.2%) and only slightly more principals indicated that music teachers are consulates but don't participate in the interviews (5.4%). Ten administrators (10.8%) indicated that they do not consult anyone else when hiring a music teacher.

Participation Rates and Offerings

When asked what percentage of their school population was enrolled in a music class, 21.5% of principals indicated that 0–20% were enrolled, 26.9% indicated that 21–40% were enrolled, 23.7% indicated that 41–60% were enrolled, 19.4% indicated that 61–80% were enrolled, and 8.6% indicated that 81–100% of their school population was enrolled. A Pearson χ^2 test of independence indicated no significant association between school locale and the percent of the school population enrolled in music courses, $\chi^2(12, n = 93) = 11.211, p = .511$. The vast majority of administrators reported that their school(s) offered concert band (91.4%) and/or concert choir (84.9%) and over 40% of the administrators who responded to the survey indicated a desire to offer piano (44.1%) and music production (40.9%) (see Table 5.1 for complete list of offerings and desired offerings).

Choir (n=31) and band (n=29) were at the top of the list of courses that administrators indicated as "must-have" classes. One administrator added, "Teachers are trained in and only interested in

Table 5.1 Listing of Music Classes and if They Are Offered or Would Like To Be Offered

	Offered	*Not offered but interested in offering*	*Not offered and no interest in offering*
Concert Band	91.4	4.3	4.3
Concert Choir	84.9	10.8	4.3
Jazz Band	50.5	31.2	18.3
Marching Band	44.1	20.4	35.5
Show Choir	35.5	34.4	30.1
Guitar	28.0	36.6	35.5
Music Theory	24.7	25.8	49.5
Orchestra	20.4	26.9	52.7
Other	15.1	9.7	75.3
AP Music Theory	12.9	17.2	69.9
Music Production	9.7	40.9	49.5
Ukulele	8.6	25.8	65.6
Piano	8.6	44.1	47.
Songwriting	2.2	34.4	63.4
Mariachi	2.2	22.6	75.3
Rock Band	1.1	38.7	60.2

Note. All values are percentages.

traditional course offerings." A few mentioned middle school general music, elementary general music, marching band, and orchestra. Other offerings with which more than one principal did not want to part were marching band (n=4) and mariachi (n=2). Three themes came to the fore as roadblocks to adding or changing courses offered: lack of staff (n=36), time/schedule (n=27), and funding (n=21). Not having enough students (n=12), student interest (n= 9), and space (n=7) were minor themes. In the case of an administrator from an urban New Jersey school, "We don't [have] enough music teachers to offer all of those courses. Also, I hadn't thought of them." Principals did, however, share some of their school's current music offerings that they had been able to work into their curriculum. These included world drumming, musical theater, history of musicals, hip-hop class, drumline, madrigal, pep band, and a musical styles and composition class. One stated they were "always open to anything music teachers want to do, yet doesn't overwhelm them professionally." Over half (59.1%) of the administrators indicated that the vision for the music program belonged to the music teacher with support from administration, 36.6% indicated it was an equally shared responsibility, and 4.3% indicated that it was the administrator's responsibility to provide the vision and the music teacher's responsibility to implement it.

Skills, Knowledge, and Dispositions

The principals were asked to rank a list of music-specific skills or knowledge from most to least important, and the ability to teach a variety of music classes was ranked as most important by 40.9% of the respondents (see Table 5.2 for complete list of skills and rankings). The ability to teach a variety of classes and the ability to conduct a large ensemble each garnered over 60% of the first and second-place votes. No significant relationship was observed between school locale and any of the music skills/knowledge areas.

Spearman's rank–order correlation was computed to assess the relationship between the various skills and knowledge ranking and, in order to avoid the increased possibility for a Type I error due to multiple pairwise comparison, the Bonferroni correction was used. A moderate, negative correlation was observed between administrators who value the ability to conduct a large ensemble and administrators who value the ability to teach a variety of classes, $\rho(92) = -.46, p < .001$.

Table 5.2 Ranking of Music Skills/Knowledge Areas

	1	*2*	*3*	*4*	*5*	*6*	*7*	*8*	*9*	*10*	*11*
Teach a variety of music classes	40.9	12.9	10.8	9.7	4.3	6.5	5.4	3.2	1.1	5.4	0.0
Conduct a large ensemble	28.0	34.4	11.8	10.8	6.5	1.1	1.1	1.1	0.0	4.3	1.1
Other	17.2	6.5	1.1	1.1	1.1	0.0	0.0	0.0	0.0	1.1	72.0
Ability on primary instrument	5.4	18.3	14.0	14.0	18.3	8.6	7.5	3.2	5.4	3.2	2.2
Play piano	4.3	7.5	14.0	4.3	19.4	16.1	16.1	6.5	6.5	3.2	2.2
Teach composition	2.2	9.7	17.2	10.8	9.7	18.3	7.5	9.7	2.2	10.8	2.2
Use technology	1.1	7.5	17.2	20.4	15.1	14.0	14.0	3.2	2.2	5.4	0.0
Teach improvisation	1.1	1.1	11.8	16.1	10.8	14.0	14.0	10.8	9.7	7.5	3.2
Teach western art music	0.0	1.1	0.0	2.2	1.1	9.7	14.0	30.1	20.4	18.3	3.2
Teach popular music	0.0	1.1	1.1	9.7	11.8	5.4	7.5	9.7	18.3	24.7	10.8
Teach jazz music	0.0	0.0	1.1	1.1	2.2	6.5	12.9	22.6	34.4	16.1	3.2

Note: All values are percentages.

A wide variety of "important qualities" or dispositions were mentioned by principals looking to hire a music educator. Several mentioned desiring a teacher who is flexible (*n*=9), organized (*n*=7), passionate (*n*=7), a willing collaborator (*n*=6), and student-centered (*n*=4). Many also mentioned the need for an energetic, engaging, and enthusiastic personality (*n*=26) and discussed recruiting and retaining or the ability to grow the program (*n*=10). The two most common themes were the ability to build relationships with students (*n*=31) and being qualified in terms of skill in the field, content knowledge, and pedagogy (*n*=30). The largest "red flag" for an administrator hiring a music educator is a job history that shows a great deal of moving from school to school (*n*=12).

Discussion

Our aim was to better understand the music positions for which administrators are hiring, as well as how administrators approach their hiring practices and what they value with respect to filling secondary level music positions. In order to do so, we examined the content of advertised openings, explored how administrators approach the interview process, and investigated personal, professional, and content-specific qualities valued by principals when hiring music educators.

Content of Advertised Openings

Job postings for music positions in these five states overwhelmingly indicated a desire to hire a BCO teacher, complicating efforts to expand the secondary curriculum. Findings corroborated those of Prendergast (2021) and Schmidt et al. (2006), who reported an abundance of job descriptions containing multiple specialties. Groulx (2016) reported 83% of music educators had taught outside their area of specialty; in this case about half of the openings described positions in which the candidate would work with students at multiple levels. The large number of combination jobs supports the need for the broad preparation described by several researchers (Greher and Tobin, 2006; Henry, 2002; May et al., 2017).

Forty percent of the job postings were for positions in rural areas. Small school music programs are often connected to community events and boast many traditions (Spring, 2013; VanDeusen, 2016); these cherished customs may result in less willingness to diversify school music offerings. Abril and Gault (2008) noted significant differences in the diversity of offerings when comparing schools in rural locations to those in suburban and urban locations. The large percentage of jobs advertised in rural areas combined with the tendency toward less diversity in offerings in these areas may further contribute to implicit standardization of school music positions.

Actual positions may contain more diverse expectations than postings revealed but, if a majority of employment options explicitly call for large ensemble specialists, it may be more challenging for music teacher educators to make compelling arguments that promote curricular change. Furthermore, administrators seem to be most concerned with serving a large number of students in their music program, the student–teacher ratio for which is most easily accomplished through large ensembles in which it is not unusual, for example, to have 50 students assigned to one teacher. Principals interviewed desired to find a teacher with the personality to grow the current program focused on large ensemble instruction and may not have even considered offerings other than band, orchestra, and choir that may attract additional students to the music program. However, as Elpus and Abril (2019) point out, increasing the diversity of music courses offered may not increase overall enrollment in a given music program if the new course offerings have a cap on the number of students that can enroll, as can be the case due to limitations of available resources.

The Interview

The initial screening of candidates, which often focuses on professional attributes gleaned from grade reports, reference letters, and documentation of practicum experiences, may or may not showcase non-traditional skills that would be valuable in teaching or creating non-traditional music offerings. Personal attributes likely do not come into play until the face-to-face interview phase (Mason & Schroeder, 2010.).

About 40% of participants used the same questions when interviewing for music positions as they do when hiring teachers for other subjects. Over 80% involve the current music teacher(s) in the process, suggesting that music educators have the opportunity to serve as a point of disruption; they have the power to hire colleagues with the skills to create more diverse offerings. Charisma, flexibility, reaching more students, and finding someone to successfully lead large ensembles were key for the principals who participated in our study. At least one of the administrators in Phase II mentioned that the same is true for teachers of other subjects to a certain degree, but that the need to recruit makes it even more important for music educators.

Personal, Professional, and Content-Specific Qualities

Similar to other findings (Doerksen and Richter, 2007; 2009; Groulx, 2016; Wilson and McGinnis, 2018) regarding music teacher educators and in-service music educators, dispositional qualities were seen as being as important or more important than musical or pedagogical skills and knowledge. The desire on the part of administrators who participated in the present study to hire music educators with the charisma to be able to grow the program as well as for the outward/community-facing aspects of the position echoed previous findings (Mason and Schroeder, 2010; Ratliff, Ratliff, & Watson, 2013) that identified enthusiasm as an important characteristic. The most important qualification described by principals was the ability to build relationships with students followed by a combination of skill in the field, content knowledge, and pedagogical knowledge.

Over 60% of our participants ranked the ability to conduct a large ensemble as either the most important or second-most important skill they believed a future music educator should possess while over 50% ranked the ability to teach a variety of music classes as either most or second-most important. There is an apparent discrepancy between the broad preparation necessary to meet the administrators' desire for music educators to teach a variety of classes and the specialized preparation needed to teach the courses that over 40% of administrators listed as "non-negotiables" (choir and band). Further, those administrators who highly valued conducting ability were significantly less likely to value the ability to teach a variety of classes, and vice versa. This suggests that there may be less uniformity in what administrators desire, which may be in part due to the disproportionate number of respondents from Minnesota.

When considering these competing desires alongside the administrators' propensity to respond to student interest and include as many students as possible in the music programs, it may actually represent an opportunity for curricular disruption. The findings of this study indicate that music teachers may have a large degree of autonomy in the music course offerings at their respective schools, as almost 60% of the Phase III administrators suggested that it is the music teacher's responsibility to provide the vision for the music program. Because administrators value the community connections and the enrollment numbers that large ensembles provide, replacing large ensembles with other offerings may not be well-received. However, the fact that non-BCO offerings do not negatively impact BCO enrollment (Powell, 2019) suggests that teachers may be able to successfully advocate for broader music course offerings at their schools. This autonomy represents exciting possibilities for K-12 music educators and course offerings.

While the possibilities for K-12 are promising, if both depth and breadth are highly valued by administrators, additional study is imperative as there are complicated implications for teacher education. In keeping with what Juchniewicz (2007) noted were challenges observed by music educators, the administrators in this study cited logistical concerns as roadblocks to offering non-BCO courses, including lack of teacher expertise. The homogeneity of both the demographic profile of music educators in the United States (Elpus, 2015) and the music teacher education curricula of NASM-accredited institutions (Talbot & Matie, 2015) likely contribute to the lack of teacher expertise with non-BCO music offerings. Findings supported the work of Teachout (1997) and Essex (2010) who suggest a "vicious cycle" of tradition in which students trained in Western European traditions become music educators in programs that were designed to train professional performers over 200 years ago. This homogeneity is a critical area of concern for those interested in curricular disruption.

Conclusion

Music teacher educators continue to be challenged by the need to prepare preservice teachers to uphold the large ensemble tradition while being broadly trained to accommodate students in a variety of settings and from a diversity of backgrounds. As Shuler (2011) suggested, one roadblock to diversifying options is simply that music program quality is sometimes seen as a numbers game. Administrators want as many students in the program as possible and large ensembles provide a way for one teacher to be with many students. Further, the community created by ensembles can be an essential piece of a student's music education but it could also be accomplished through multiple small ensembles in a single class, reaching more students than would a teacher offering private or small group lessons to ensemble members, as is often the case in Iowa, for example (Prendergast, 2021). Even within large ensemble offerings, members of the profession might continue to look for ways to diversify the pedagogical approaches employed (Heuser, 2015).

Additional research is needed to determine to what degree administrators, communities, students, K-12 music educators, and other stakeholders are interested in curricular change. Administrators may be open to new possibilities but may not be aware of what those possibilities could be, much less be concerned with the philosophical and social implications of only offering large ensemble music education. Intentional disruption is necessary to bring about change due to the reifying nature of public school music education, music teacher education, and music teacher hiring practices. There may simply be a lack of familiarity with curricular possibilities that provide a music education aimed at being inclusive of more students. Further examination regarding the onus put on young teachers at the beginning of their careers would also be valuable – including the examining and encouraging of teacher agency – as would the continued consideration of the skills preservice music educators need beyond the current focus on the Western European tradition given that the skill set of the teacher hired is an important factor. Suggestions for future research also include a need to both determine and problematize student interest.

Action Steps

Current music educators:

- Encourage school districts to formulate job descriptions when advertising for open positions that accurately reflect all of the job responsibilities, including those non-BCO responsibilities, in order to help administrators determine how important breadth versus depth of given skills are for a given position and allow the applicant pool to communicate their appropriateness for a given position earlier in the application process.
- Advocate for new course offerings. Curricular disruption can occur in the large ensemble through varied pedagogical approaches not

traditionally employed in BCO classes, or through offering new music classes not previously offered at a given school, especially when driven by student interest. Recommending and implementing new courses can feel daunting but given the logistical challenges that often serve as roadblocks for these endeavors problem-solving those challenges and offering solutions as you make the case for new classes may help persuade skeptical administrators.

Future music educators:

- Communicate enthusiasm for the subject, as well as concrete ideas for recruiting students to music classes during the interview. Doing so will likely be compelling to principals and others involved in hiring decisions. Administrators are looking for personal qualities that will draw students to their music programs and demonstrating that you have both the personal dispositions and broad content expertise to draw students in will likely be compelling to potential employers.
- Broaden your musical engagement to include listening to and performing genres you have previously had little experience with to grow your musical skills and confidence. Administrators value both depth and breadth of skills, depending on the positions for which they're hiring.

Music teacher educators:

- Offer workshops and certification programs to help prepare current music educators to both teach and advocate for new course offerings.
- Create community-based programs that provide service learning opportunities as well as models for offerings outside of band, orchestra and choir. Inviting local students to be part of a six-week modern band class, for example, could be a great learning environment for both the young students and the preservice educators.
- Dream about and propose curriculum changes. Start having conversations with music faculty colleagues about the demands of music education in the 21st century. Ask the hard questions; for example, what might we give up to make way for a focus on creating more inclusive music programs?

Administrators:

- Craft job descriptions that include possibilities for duties beyond large ensemble instruction. Doing so may open attractive opportunities for your teachers to play to their strengths and interests.
- Support teachers in pursuing professional development. Many music educators have been trained to teach secondary level music primarily through large ensemble instruction rather than receiving the breadth of knowledge necessary to serve as the only music teacher in a building, or to teach more than a specific large ensemble class. Content-specific professional development opportunities may be especially important for music teachers in small and/or rural schools where these opportunities may be even more limited.
- Advocate for scheduling and resources to support innovative teachers and course offerings.
- Share enthusiasm for including as many students as possible in music education!

References

Abril, C. R., & Gault, B. M. (2008). The state of music in secondary schools: The principal's perspective. *Journal of Research in Music Education*, *56*(1), 68–81. https://doi.org/10.1177/0022429408317516

Bolz, A. J. (2009). *Screening teacher candidates: Luck of the draw or objective selection?* (Publication No. 3367803) [Doctoral dissertation, University of Wisconsin, Madison]. ProQuest Dissertations & Theses Global.

Button, S. (2010). Music teachers' perceptions of effective teaching. *Bulletin for the Council of Research in Music Education*, *183*(Winter), 25–38. www.jstor.org/stable/27861470

Byo, J. (2018). "Modern Band" as school music: A case study. *International Journal of Music Education*, *36*(2), 259–269. https://doi.org/10.1177/0255761417729546

Colley B. (2009). Educating teachers to transform the trilogy. *Journal of Music Teacher Education*, *19*(1), 56–67. https://doi.org/10.1177%2F1057083709344042

Conway, C. M. (2012). Ten years later: Teachers reflect on "perceptions of beginning teachers, their mentors, and administrator regarding preservice music teacher preparation." *Journal of Research in Music Education*, *60*(3), 324–338. https://doi.org/10.1177/0022429412453601

Council of Chief State School Officers (CCSSO) Interstate Teacher Assessment and Support Consortium (InTASC) (2013). InTASC Model Core Teaching

Standards and Learning Progressions for Teachers 1.0. https://ccsso.org/sites/default/files/2017-12/2013_INTASC_Learning_Progressions_for_Teachers.pdf

Creswell, J. W. (2014). *Research design: qualitative, quantitative, and mixed methods approaches* (4th ed). Sage.

Culp, M. E., & Clauhs, M. (2020). Factors that affect participation in secondary school music: reducing barriers and increasing access. *Music Educators Journal*, *106*(4): 43–49. https://doi.org/10.1177/0027432120918293

Doerksen, P., & Ritcher, G. (2007, September). *The 2007 survey of music teacher certification programs*. Paper presented at the Symposium on Music Teacher Education, Greensboro, NC.

Doerksen, P., & Ritcher, G. (2009, September). *The assessment of professional dispositions in music teacher certification programs*. Paper presented at the Symposium on Music Teacher Education, Greensboro, NC.

Elpus, K. (2015). Music teacher licensure candidates in the United States: A demographic profile and analysis of licensure examination scores. *Journal of Research in Music Education*, *63*(3), 314–335. https://doi.org/10.1177/0022429415602470

Elpus, K., & Abril, C. R. (2011). High school music ensemble students in the United States: A demographic profile. *Journal of Research in Music Education*, *59*(2), 128–145. https://doi.org/10.1177/0022429411405207

Elpus, K., & Abril, C. R. (2019). Who enrolls in high school music? A national profile of U.S. students, 2009–2013. *Journal of Research in Music Education*, *67*(3) 323–338.

Engel, M. (2013). Problematic preferences? A mixed method examination of principals' preferences for teacher characteristics in Chicago. *Educational Administration Quarterly*, *49*(1), 52–92. https://doi.org/10.1177/0013161X12451025

Engel, M., & Curran, F. C. (2016). Toward understanding principals' hiring practices, *Journal of Educational Administration*, *54*(2), 173–190. https://doi.org/10.1108/JEA-04-2014-0049

Essex, M. W. (2010). *The dialectic of modernization: Implications for music teacher education* [Doctoral dissertation, Ohio State University]. OhioLINK Electronic Theses and Dissertations Center. http://rave.ohiolink.edu/etdc/view?acc_num=osu1274451516

Freer, P. K. (2011). The performance-pedagogy paradox in choral music teaching. *Philosophy of Music Education Review*, *19*(2), 164–178. https://doi.org/10.2979/philmusieducrevi.19.2.164

Give a Note Foundation. (2017). *The status of music education in United States public schools-2017.* Reston, VA. www.giveanote.org/initiatives/research-findings-on-the-status-of-music-education-in-u-s-public-schools/

Greher, G. R., & Tobin, R. N. (2006). Taking the long view toward music teacher preparation: The rationale for a dual degree program. *Music Educators Journal, 92*(5), 50–55. https://doi.org/10.2307/3878503

Groulx, T. (2016). Perceptions of course value and issues of specialization in undergraduate music teacher education curricula. *Journal of Music Teacher Education, 25*(2) 13–24. https://doi.org/10.1177/1057083714564874

Hamann, D. L., Lineburgh, N., & Paul, S. (1998). Teaching effectiveness and social skill development. *Journal of Research in Music Education, 46*(1), 87–101. www.jstor.org/stable/3345762

Harris, N. Rutledge, S., Ingle, W., & Thompson, C. (2010). Mix and match: What principals really look for when hiring teachers. *Education Finance and Policy, 5*(2), 228–246. www.jstor.org/stable/10.2307/educf inapoli.5.2.228

Hash, P. M. (2021). Student retention in school bands and orchestras: A literature review. *Update: Applications of research in music education.* Advanced online publication. https://doi.org/10.1177/87551233211042585

Henry, M. L. (2005). An analysis of certification practices for music education in the fifty states. *Journal of Music Teacher Education, 14*(2), 47–61. http://dx.doi.org/10.1177/10570837050140020108

Heuser, F. (2015). Pipe dreams, ideals and transformation in music education: Lessons from the field. *Research Studies in Music Education, 37*(2), 215–231. https://doi.org/10.1177/1231103X15614322

Hickey, M., & Rees, F. (2002). Developing a model for change in music teacher education. *Journal of Music Teacher Education, 12*(1), 1. https://doi.org/10.1177/10570837020120010701

Hourigan, R., & Scheib, J. (2009). Inside and outside the undergraduate music curriculum. *Journal of Music Teacher Education, 18*(2), 48–61.

Hughes, T. R. (2014). Hiring at risk: Time to ensure hiring really is the most important thing we do. *NCPEA International Journal of Educational Leadership Preparation, 9*(1), 90–102.

Jones, P. (2008). Preparing music teachers for change: Broadening instrument class offerings to foster lifewide and lifelong musicing. *Visions of Research in Music Education, 12*, 1–15. http://users.rider.edu/~vrme/v12n1/vision/2%20AERA%20-%20Jones.pdf

Juchniewicz, J. (2007). Band directors' preferences and attitudes on the implementation of non-traditional music classes. *Research Perspectives in Music Education, 11*(1), 6–11.

Kelly, S. N., & Veronee, K. (2019). High school students' perceptions of non-traditional music classes. *Bulletin of the Council for Research in Music Education, 219*, 77–89. https://doi.org/10.5406/bulcouresmusedu.219.0077

Kersten, T. (2008). Teacher hiring practices: Illinois principals' perspectives. *The Educational Forum, 72*(4), 355–368.

Kimpton, J. (2005). What to do about music teacher education: Our profession at a crossroads. *Journal of Music Teacher Education*, *14*(2), 8–21. https://doi.org/10.1177/10570837050140020103

Kono, C. D. (2010). Professional traits and skills: First-year teachers principals like to hire. *Journal of College Teaching & Learning*, *7*(3), 59–64. https://doi.org/10.19030/tlc.v7i3.104

Leonhard, C. (1991). *The status of arts education in American public schools*. Report on a survey conducted by the National Arts Education Research Center at the University of Illinois. Council for Research in Music Education, School of Music, University of Illinois at Urbana-Champaign.

Liu, E., & Johnson, S. M. (2006). New teachers' experiences of hiring: Late, rushed, and information-poor. *Educational Administration Quarterly*, *42*(3), 324–360. https://doi.org/10.1177/0013161X05282610

Madsen, C. K., Standley, J. M., Byo, J., & Cassidy, J. W. (1992). Assessment of effective teaching by instrumental music student teachers and experts. *Update: Applications of Research in Music Education*, *10*(2), 20–24.

Mantie, R., Gulish, S., McCandless, G., Solis, T., & Williams, D. (2017). Creating music curricula of the future: Preparing undergraduate music students to engage. College Music Society Symposium: Exploring Diverse Perspectives, Sept. 27, 2017. https://doi.org/10.18177/sym.2017.57.fr.11357

Mason, R., & Schroeder, M. (2010). Principal hiring practices: Toward a reduction of uncertainty. *The Clearing House*, *83*, 186–193.

May, B., Willie, K., Worthen, C., & Pehrson, A. (2017). An analysis of state music education certification and licensure practices in the United States. *Journal of Music Teacher Education*, *27*(1), 65–88. https://doi.org/10.1177/1057083717699650

Miksza, P., Roeder, M., & Biggs, D. (2010). Surveying Colorado band directors' opinions of skills and characteristics important to successful music teaching. *Journal of Research in Music Education*, *57*(4), 364–381.

Peterson, K. D. (2002). *Effective teacher hiring: A guide to getting the best*. Association of Supervision and Curriculum Development.

Powell, B. (2019). A zero-sum game? Modern bands impact on student enrollment in traditional music ensembles. *School Music News*. https://digitalcommons.montclair.edu/cgi/viewcontent.cgi?article=1041&context=cali-facpubs

Powell, B., Smith, G. D., West, C., & Kratus, J. (2019). Popular music education: A call to action. *Music Educators Journal*, *106*(1), 21–24. https://doi.org/10.1177/0027432119861528

Prendergast, J. S. (2021). Music education and music educators in Missouri, Iowa, and Illinois. *Journal of Research in Music Education*, *69*(2), 228–243. https://doi.org/10.1177/0022429420961501

Ratliff, L., Ratliff J., & Watson, P. (2013) Public school principals' perceptions concerning the hiring of social studies teachers. *The Councilor: A Journal of the Social Studies*, *74*(1), 11–24.

Rohwer, D., & Henry, W. (2004). University teachers' perceptions of requisite skills and characteristics of effective music teachers. *Journal of Music Teacher Education, 13*(2), 18–27. https://doi.org/10.1177/10570837040130020104

Royston, N. S., & Springer, D. G. (2015). Beliefs of applied studio faculty on desirable traits of prospective music education majors: A pilot study. *Journal of Music Teacher Education*, *25*(1): 78–94. https://doi.org/10.1177/1057083714549467

Royston, N. S., & Wilson, J. (2022) Dispositional and trait perceptions and beliefs: A snapshot of three stakeholders. *Visions of Research in Music Education, 39*(7). https://digitalcommons.lib.uconn.edu/vrme/vol39/iss1/7

Sanderson, D. N. (2014). *Music class offerings beyond bands, choirs, and orchestras in Nebraska high schools.* [Master's Thesis, University of Nebraska]. Student Research, Creative Activity, and Performance – School of Music. http://digitalcommons.unl.edu/musicstudent/78

Sarath, E., Myers, D., & Shehan Campbell, P. (2017*)*. Transforming music study from its foundations: A manifesto for progressive change in the undergraduate preparation of music majors. In E. Sarath, D. Myers, & P. Shehan Campbell (Eds.), *Redefining Music Studies in an Age of Change: Creativity, Diversity, and Integration* (pp. 45–85). Routledge.

Schmidt, C. P., Baker, E., Hayes, B., & Kwan, E. (2006). A descriptive study of public school music programs in Indiana. *Bulletin of the Council for Research in Music Education*, *169*, 25–37. www.jstor.org/stable/40319308

Seidman, I. (2019). *Interviewing as qualitative research* (5th ed.). Teachers College Press.

Shuler, S. (2011). Building inclusive, effective, twenty-first-century music programs. *Music Educators Journal*, *98*(1), 8–13. https://doi.org/10.1177/0027432111418748

Spring, J. (2013). Perspectives of a rural music educator: A narrative journey through 'sense of place.' *Rural Educator, 34*(3), 27–37. https://doi.org/10.35608/ruraled.v34i3.397

Strauss, R. P. (1999). Who gets hired to teach? The case of Pennsylvania. In M. Kanstoroom & C.E. Finn (Eds.), *Better teachers, better schools* (pp. 103–130). Thomas B. Fordham Foundation.

Talbot, B. C., & Mantie, R. (2015). Vision and the legitimate order: Theorizing today to imagine tomorrow. In S. W. Conkling (Ed.), *Envisioning music teacher education* (pp. 155–180). Rowman & Littlefield.

Teachout, D. (2005). From the chair: How are we preparing the next generation of music educators? *Journal of Music Teacher Education*, *15*(1), 3–5. https://doi.org/10.1177/1057083710377722

Teachout, D. J. (1997). Preservice and experienced teachers' opinions of skills and behaviors important to successful music teaching. *Journal of Research in Music Education, 45* (1), 41–50.

Thornton, L., Murphy, P., & Hamilton, S. (2004). A case of faculty collaboration for music education curricular change. *Journal of Music Teacher Education, 13*(2), 34–40. https://doi.org/10.1177/10570837040130020106

VanDeusen, A. (2016). "It really comes down to the community": A case study of a rural school music program. *Action, Criticism, & Theory in Music Education, 15*(4), 56–75. doi:10.22176/act15.4.56

Wayman, V. E. (2006). Beginning music education students' and student teachers' opinions of skills and behaviors important to successful music teaching. *Contributions to Music Education, 33*, 29–42.

Williams, D. B. (2007, June 25–29). *Reaching the "other 80%:" Using technology to engage "nontraditional music students" in creative activities* [Conference presentation]. Tanglewood II "Technology and Music Education" Symposium. Minneapolis, Minnesota. https://musiccreativity.org/documents/tanglewood2tech_dbwilliams0.pdf

Williams, D. B. (2019). *A different paradigm in music education: Re-examining the Profession*. Routledge.

Wilson, J., & McGinnis, E. (2018). A comparison of music faculty and music education faculty beliefs regarding music curricula for pre-service teachers. *Visions of Research in Music Education, 32*(8). https://digitalcommons.lib.uconn.edu/vrme/vol32/iss1/8

Yin, R. K. (2018). *Case study research and applications*, Vol. 6. Sage.

Younker, B. A., & Hickey, M. (2007). Examining the profession through the lens of social justice: Two music educators' stories and their stark realizations. *Music Education Research, 9*(2), 215–227. https://doi.org/10.1080/14613800701384334

6 Disrupting Professional Development for Music Educators

Transformations through a Five-Layer Teacher-Centric Paradigm

Daniel C. Johnson

Introduction/Overview

Professional development (PD) is a standard expectation, and requirement, for every P-12 teacher's professional growth throughout the span of their career (Kennedy, 2016). To be effective, PD engages teachers as both learners and teachers; ideally, it should expand their understanding of the learning and teaching processes, as well as their knowledge of the students they teach (Darling-Hammond, 1995). Because teacher quality is arguably the single most important factor influencing whether students learn and improve academically (Hattie, 2009; Kane & Staiger, 2008), effective PD is essential to successful teaching and learning. Targeted teacher PD, focused on key pedagogical skills (Simonsen et al., 2020), is the best way to reach individual teachers and assist them in improving their expertise and related student learning outcomes (Desimone et al., 2013; Lai & McNaughton, 2016; Meissel et al., 2016). Applications of targeted PD directly address both content and the delivery mode to provide interactive and meaningful professional learning (Desimone, 2009, 2011).

The research literature on general teacher PD has not yielded many actionable steps to assist teachers in improving their actual instructional practices or measurable student learning outcomes (Darling-Hammond et al., 2009). Assimilating this literature is problematic because it reflects multiple and often competing priorities from agencies at different administrative levels. More importantly, the assumptions that contrasting PD approaches make about teacher

DOI: 10.4324/9781003410645-6

knowledge and skills are often tacit and conflict with each other (Bautista et al., 2017; Buchanan et al., 2022). One analysis of empirical research, however, has distilled five features of effective PD: content focused, active learning, coherence, duration, and collaborative participation (Desimone, 2011). As explored below, this perspective on general teacher PD provides an important lens through which to disrupt music teacher PD.

Arts education, and specifically music education, is one of the few areas that promotes student achievement broadly and school-wide; students who enjoy wide-ranging and high-quality arts education have a lower drop-out rate, earn higher test scores, and develop 21st century skills for life (Johnson & Howell, 2009; Noblit et al., 2000; Noblit et al., 2009). Those skills, such as critical and creative thinking, perseverance, and problem-solving, boost their achievement in other subject areas. When their teachers benefit from effective PD, students directly reap the rewards. They have more efficient and satisfied teachers who successfully deploy ambitious and innovative teaching strategies that augment learning (Bautista & Ortega-Ruíz, 2015; Darling-Hammond, 1995). As such, quality music teacher PD in all areas is essential to improving instruction, providing benefits to both teachers and their P-12 students (Koner & Eros, 2019). Despite the widespread agreement that PD improves teachers' knowledge and skills in order to improve student learning (Bautista & Ortega-Ruíz, 2015; Darling-Hammond et al., 2009), specialist teachers experience the confluence of competing PD priorities as promoted by different stakeholders (Buchanan et al., 2022). As a result, they often perceive their school and district-level PD experiences, which regularly focus on generic instructional practices or learning in more traditionally academic disciplines, as irrelevant and ineffective (Bautista et al., 2017).

As a reflection of the increased interest in research on music teacher PD, the *Journal of Music Teacher Education* in 2007 and *Arts Education Policy Review* in 2011 both devoted special issues to this topic. Building upon those ideas, this chapter amplifies emergent trends in the literature to introduce a teacher-centric paradigm on disrupting ineffective music teacher PD while simultaneously promoting teacher motivation, perceived needs, and relevant topics (Bautista et al., 2018; West et al., 2022). This disruption is important because it directly affects the professional lives of thousands of school music teachers who are required to complete their annual PD hours for recertification despite persistent complaints that those hours are irrelevant or perfunctory (Kennedy, 2016). As discussed below, this disruption also promotes best practices in music teacher PD as long-term programs that offer choices and honor teacher expertise. In addition, the resulting new paradigm facilitates mentorship, is site-specific, promotes self-reflection, and is musical (Bautista et al., 2017; Desimone, 2009, 2011; NAfME, 2015a).

Examining the research on PD in music teacher education provides a basis for the disruptions to music teacher PD proposed in this chapter. After exploring those ideas, a section displaying and discussing the new paradigm as points of disruption follows. To conclude this chapter, example applications and action steps extend these ideas before this chapter closes with implications and a forward-thinking trajectory.

Professional Development for Music Teachers

An overview of related research literature on music teacher PD provides an understanding of traditional thought and practices – traditions that themselves provide the most compelling need for disruptions to professional practices. To move beyond prescriptive formats of traditional PD where "one size fits all" (Darling-Hammond et al., 2009), music teacher-educators have recently advocated for PD that emphasizes collaboration and reflection, as well as inquiry and synthesis (e.g. Campbell, 2014; Rickels & Brewer, 2017; Stanley et al., 2014; Upitis & Brook, 2017). Other music education scholars have further indicated that differentiated offerings according to teaching experience and context are essential factors for effective PD (Bauer, 2007; Conway, 2001; Desimone & Garet, 2015; Draves, 2017; Eros, 2011, 2013).

Overall, however, the research literature on music teacher PD is fragmented and reveals several shortcomings. Namely, that most related research focuses on PD effects instead of its processes (Bautista & Ortega-Ruíz, 2015) and lacks robust theoretical frameworks (West et al., 2021). While also lagging behind other topics in the field (Bush, 2007), research on music teacher PD most often measures PD in terms of quantity instead of quality (Good & Lavinge, 2017). In addressing the absence of a valid measure for PD quality, Wesolowski et al. (2021) determined that PD for music teachers is largely content-specific and standards-based but is routinely short-term and not collaborative.

The main problem, however, with conventional PD for music teachers is relevance. This, along with the related lack of engagement and teacher buy-in, prevent it from fulfilling its potential to improve teacher practices and student learning. Conventional PD often takes the form of pre-packaged "advice from experts" and ineffective, one-off workshops focused on trying to make teachers teach better (Kennedy, 2016). As reported by Bush (2007), Hammel (2007), and Rolandson and Ross-Hekkel (2002), music teachers generally do not recognize how such PD offerings connect with them professionally. Related to relevance is the issue of engagement, or more accurately disengagement. Participation in PD simply to fulfill state-mandated hours does not translate into actual results, i.e., professional growth and development (Hill, 2009). In terms of content knowledge, pedagogical knowledge, and pedagogical content knowledge (Millican, 2008), music teachers need to maintain and balance all three knowledge bases while applying them to a wide range of P-12 learners. Disruptions to the current PD offering for music teachers focus on both musical content and its delivery in a wide range of P-12 settings.

A music teacher–centric PD paradigm aims to disrupt the habitual content and customary delivery of routine PD by being both content and context-specific. It addresses the lack of relevance and engagement in prescribed PD format. In addition, it offers sustained results for P-12 music teachers throughout their career cycle, an important facet for meaningful and effective PD (Johnson et al., 2019; Koner & Eros, 2019). Such a new paradigm is also teacher-centric, built from the bottom-up, and highlights teacher strengths. In particular, PD that begins from teachers' perspectives and addresses their concerns and aspirations is likely to be more relevant than training developed from administrative priorities. A bottom-up design with its inherent authority from first-hand experience (Darling-Hammond, 1990), builds PD from teachers' actual practice and practical realities while also disrupting the top-down model of district or school-wide mandates and "teacher trainings" during which "one size fits all" (Darling-Hammond et al., 2009; Hill, 2009). In addition, this type of bottom-up, collegial PD builds on teachers' strengths and expands their competencies while increasing professional confidence (Darling-Hammond & McLaughlin, 1995), instead of focusing on their weaknesses via deficit models (e.g. Danielson, 2013). Furthermore, because music teachers influence the PD content and design, teacher-centric PD builds teacher agency in ways similar to those investigated among preservice teachers by Tucker (2020).

Points of Disruption

Developed with an understanding of P-12 teacher perspectives on and experiences with PD, Five Layers of Relevance have emerged from previous literature (Johnson et al., 2019; Wesolowski et al., 2021). The idea of teacher experience being the source of knowledge is not new; decades ago, Schwab (1959/1978) described this idea to honor teachers as agents of education. In the years since, PD has at times become more focused on teacher deficits and judgmental feedback from administrators (Danielson, 2013). Therefore, this disruption to music teacher PD represents a paradigm shift. As shown in Figure 6.1, this paradigm has five aspects or layers that define and describe its relevance to in-service P-12 music teachers.

In order to signal differences in specialist teachers' needs, the layers of relevance are parallel to but slightly different from those established for general teacher PD (Desimone, 2011). These five layers are inclusive of diverse cultures because they acknowledge the effects of musical culture, experience, geography, learners' development, and pedagogy on effective and relevant PD. The diversity encompassed by these five layers is considerable, as is its potential for positively impacting PD for music teachers.

Bautista et al. (2017) examined trends in 24 music teacher PD initiatives in terms of the five characteristics of effective PD from the general education literature, i.e., content focus, active learning,

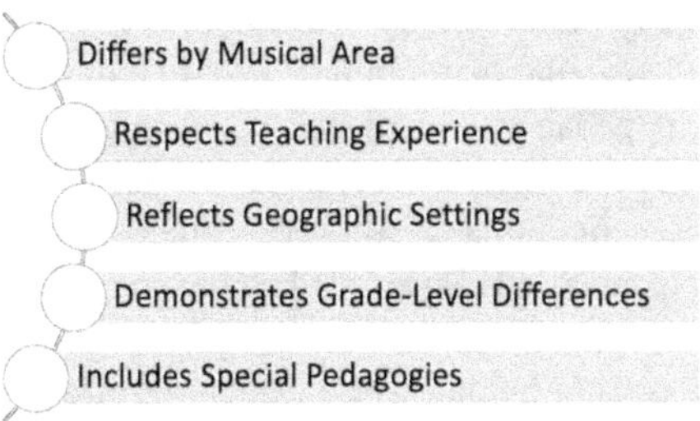

Figure 6.1 Five Layers of Relevance in Disruptive Music Teacher PD.

collective participation, duration, and coherence (Desimone, 2011). In their insightful literature review, Bautista and colleagues found that music teacher PD satisfied most of the effective PD characteristics, with three weaknesses; it did not effectively measure efficacy in terms of student achievement, promote research and writing opportunities for teachers, or provide support following PD events. While the lack of accountability in terms of student achievement presents a demonstrated threat to funding for music education programs (Fermanich, 2011), connecting these areas for improvement provides an opportunity by organizing follow-up sessions to support teachers as action researchers and curriculum authors with the focus on enhancing students' musical thinking and achievement. By combining the five features of effective PD in general education (Desimone, 2011) with the best practices for music teacher education (Bautista et al., 2017; NAfME, 2015a), a disruptive model offers multiple ways to deliver meaningful and relevant PD for music teachers in multiple contexts and career stages. Connections between these aspects of general and music teacher are shown in Figure 6.2. They lead to disruptive music teacher PD described by five disruptive characteristics, shown in Figure 6.1 as Five Layers of Relevance.

Applications and Action Steps

The points of disruption identified in this chapter transform prescribed PD for music educators into music teacher–centric programs, based on the related research literature. The need for music teacher–centric PD applies to P-12 music education in all settings. While this disruptive PD approach is context-specific, it applies to a wide range of music teaching settings. For example, although elementary general music was the setting for one pilot study in teacher-centric PD (Johnson & Stanley, 2021), later settings expanded to include P-12 music educators from a particular geographic context (Johnson et al., 2021) by using "critical pedagogy of place" (Gruenewald, 2003). In addition to teaching and geographic settings, teacher-centric PD also acknowledges and accommodates teachers' career stages as an important PD attribute (Conway & Edgar, 2014; Johnson et al., 2019). Particular settings such as teaching context, geography, and career stage are all important considerations when designing effective PD for music educators (Campbell & Barrett, 2013; Hartz et al., 2014; Reynolds et al., 2010).

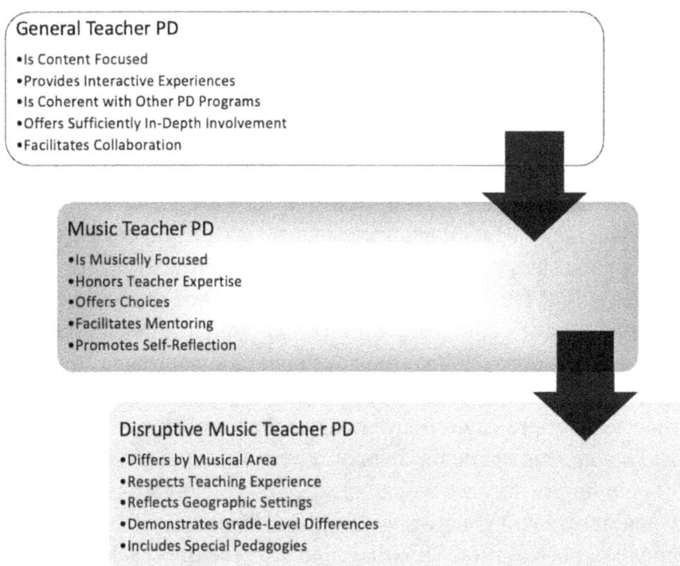

Figure 6.2 Disruptive Music Educator PD as a Teacher-Centric Paradigm.

Action steps include beginning with locally organized, teacher-centric PD to focus on specific teaching, geographic, or career stage contexts. Intermediate steps are to implement teacher-centric models based on proof-of-concept designs at the district level. Aspirational steps are to develop and adopt models that transform prescribed PD into teacher-centric professional learning experiences at the state and national levels. Expected results are enhanced teacher self-efficacy, greater student engagement, and meaningful curricular innovations.

Applications of the Five Layers of Relevance model could take many forms. Some recommendations are:

- Musical Area: working with teachers in the same musical area allows for specific pedagogical and equipment discussions related to traditional general, instrumental, and choral music teaching areas, as well as non-traditional and teaching contexts. Example PD includes general music teacher workshops designed to share understandings about contrasting elementary pedagogies (e.g., Orff-Schulwerk, Kodály, and Dalcroze); brainstorming sessions for instrumental music directors to increase student interest in joining band or choir at the middle school level; and a choral music workshop focused on the musical and pedagogical topics identified in a needs-assessment.

- Teaching Experience: networking organized according to teacher experience, such as beginning, early career, mid-career, and veteran teaching stages, facilitates career-level conversations that extend beyond the classroom. Example PD includes Professional Learning Communities (PLCs) for music teachers in the same career stage who may have common questions and similar areas for growth; mentoring programs that pair veteran and experienced music teachers so that they can share what they have learned (either from their teacher-preparation programs or their teaching experiences); and connecting music teachers on a personal level to build a sense of community and to develop unexpected collaborations.
- Geographic Setting: networking with teachers in similar geographic contexts, such as rural, suburban, and urban settings, acknowledges the importance of place and its influence on pedagogy. Example PD includes PLCs with a focus on identifying the challenges presented by teaching locations. These discussions and focus groups counteract assumptions and stereotypes about corresponding types of communities while motivating teachers to problem-solve through networking.
- Grade Level: because music teaching spans the P-12 gamut, sharing pedagogical ideas and instructional strategies specific to and across grade levels is another way to increase the impact of networking and the relevance of PD. Example PD includes sharing practical, pedagogical strategies that best suit learners at different developmental levels. Such PD with a grade-level focus is important because learners undergo multiple developmental stages that affect their cognitive, affective, and psychomotor capacities.
- Special Pedagogies: collaborations based on the wide range of special pedagogical topics, such as grant writing, advocacy and recruitment, interdisciplinary learning, Title I, ESL/ELL, and COVID-era teaching, further connect teachers who have similar interests, challenges, and/or solutions related to these topics. Example PD incorporates strategies and approaches from other educational specialties (such as exceptional children) in ways that lie within the

music teacher's comfort zone. Applying skills and knowledge from other disciplines such as music therapy could benefit students from a social-and-emotional learning perspective, while community development skills could forward grantsmanship.

Other action steps could provide alternatives to the current online PD options that regularly neglect music education. Commercial PD services offer online PD but with many shortcomings. Their main drawback is one-way delivery of prescribed PD content that does not create community, allow for flexibility, promote reflective thinking, or discussion of teachers' professional contexts (Darling-Hammond & McLaughlin, 1995). This type of PD often uses patterned and predictable modules, resulting in little, if any, lasting effects or real value for the cost (Darling-Hammond, 2010; Odden et al., 2002). Another disadvantage of these offerings is the lack of music-specific content. When music teachers find and pursue content-specific PD, they regularly encounter barriers such as cost and time commitment (Bowles, 2002). Digital networking via virtual PLCs or Virtual Professional Learning Communities (VLPCs), however, provides flexible and tailored options for teachers to share solutions and discuss challenges (Tobias, 2014). These digital networking tools can also keep teachers connected throughout the school year, with free and accessible ways to collaborate synchronously or asynchronously. Using VPLCs specifically for music teachers also counteracts the experience of professional isolation that music teachers report and addresses the "one-size-fits-all" model for school-wide PD (Bautista et al., 2017; Bautista et al., 2018; Hill, 2009; Wesolowski et al., 2021). Furthermore, innovative administrators and arts coordinators could also use VPLCs to connect their teachers using the Five Layers of Relevance.

During the COVID-19 pandemic, music teachers' interest in and readiness for PD shifted, demonstrating their motivations for effective and context-specific PD as delivered via innovative platforms (West et al., 2022). In particular, VPLCs emerged as one solution for music teacher PD in rural communities, on a national scale (Rolandson & Ross-Hekkel, 2022). Another example VPLC incorporating the Layers of Relevance was an online, focused, and flexible music teacher–centric PD course as a pilot project (Johnson & Stanley, 2021). Structured as a content and context-specific, five-week course, this project disrupted the habitual content and customary delivery of routine PD. Using a bottom-up approach, based on a first-hand understanding and experience of teaching actual P-12 students (Darling-Hammond, 1990), together with a non-hierarchical design, project facilitators engaged teacher-participants with interactive and multidirectional discussions, based on related research. As a proof-of-concept, dozens of participating music teachers reported finding solutions to their instructional and pedagogical dilemmas, while capitalizing on their expertise and increasing their self-efficacy (Johnson et al., 2021). Instead of trying to make teachers teach better, this project transformed music teacher PD by addressing the lack of relevance and engagement in traditional, prescribed PD formats. This model offers the opportunity to refine, test, and share benefits from a uniquely specific and focused model of online, focused, and flexible music teacher PD (Johnson et al., 2019; Johnson et al., 2021; Johnson & Stanley, 2021).

The goal of disrupting conventional music teacher PD is to capitalize on teacher expertise and to promote teachers' own aspirations toward self-efficacy while finding solutions to their self-identified instructional and pedagogical dilemmas. Enhanced by and based on well-established tenets of positive and educational psychology, this approach assists P-12 music teachers in developing their own teaching and learning potentials through meaningful and relevant PD. Using research-based andragogy updated for 21st century adult learners (Blackley & Sheffield, 2015), disruptive music teacher PD promotes teachers recognizing, celebrating, and expanding their collective group wisdom. Such approaches use the techniques of Core Reflection (Korthagen et al., 2012) and Knowledge Communities (Craig, 2009) to foster individual teacher growth. In addition to honoring teachers' experience, these courses incorporate content and context-specific foci. In a non-hierarchical model, this type of PD also encourages teacher-participants to recognize and expand their own professional potentials through multidirectional engagement. In addition, disrupting music teacher PD provides ways to directly address the second strategic direction of the National Association for Music Education (NAfME) – Leading the Profession – by providing "dynamic and effective learning opportunities" for music teachers nationwide (section b, NAfME, 2015b), and builds upon current work in the Area for Strategic Planning and Action (ASPA) of the Society for Music Teacher Education: Professional Development for Music Teachers.

Conclusion and Future Trajectory

Disrupting traditional practices of music teacher PD provides opportunities as new trajectories for action by teachers, supervisors, and other stakeholders. Along those pathways, teachers can more easily engage in meaningful reciprocal learning about topics most relevant to them. This type of PD has the potential to inspire and motivate music teachers to innovate and renew their pedagogical practices. As such, it is an essential part of teacher renewal and growth. Beyond the state-level mandates for regular recertification, relevant music teacher PD has the potential to shape the future of the profession and, therefore, the musical horizons of P-12 students.

Through well-established tenets of positive and educational psychology (e.g., Core Reflection and Knowledge Communities), teachers can capitalize on their own expertise and share that wisdom with their peers. Instead of highlighting deficits, this approach promotes professional aspirations and self-efficacy. In this way, teachers recognize, celebrate, and expand their own collective group wisdom. Their experience, subject expertise, and place-based pedagogy provide a foundation to enhance content and context-specific instruction. By capitalizing on these aspects of the teacher-centric PD model, the profession may take steps to improve teachers' professional capacities and teacher retention, two outcomes identified by Schmidt and Robbins in their strategic architecture for music teacher PD (2011).

Another wide-ranging implication for the profession brought about by disrupting music teacher PD is financial. Each year, millions of American public school teachers complete required PD hours for recertification at an annual cost of $18 billion (Horn & Goldstein, 2018), despite persistent complaints that those hours are irrelevant or perfunctory (Kennedy, 2016). The annual cost of PD to schools and school districts is substantial, especially when factoring in costs often excluded for PD programs themselves, i.e., the teachers' time; follow-up training and coaching; program administration; materials, equipment, and facilities; and travel (Odden et al., 2002). Therefore, the consequences of poorly designed PD include substantial costs for schools nationwide, not only in terms of teacher disinterest and perceived irrelevance, but also as more obvious financial expenditures (Hill, 2009). Especially for struggling schools that play important and multi-faceted social and educational roles, these implications are significant (Darling-Hammond et al., 2022; Odden et al., 2002).

This teacher-centric, disruptive paradigm offers innovative and effective music teacher PD with wide-ranging implications for the profession. Teachers' interests and self-perceived PD needs should be the main focus for meaningful professional growth and development (Bautista et al., 2018). As they wrote, "…for PD to be meaningful and transformative, it needs to be designed *in response to* [emphasis in original] teachers' own motivations, needs, and preferences" (p. 197). Teacher motivation, in particular, is an under-researched and influential aspect of PD, both for music and general educators alike (West et al., 2022). Transformative disruptions to pre-packaged PD begin there and honor teachers as learners throughout their career cycle. The flexibility of this approach, both in terms of delivery mode and content, provides effective and relevant PD to the broadest possible range of music teachers, accommodating their professional settings and needs. The significant financial costs associated with poorly designed and ineffective PD are a drain on scarce resources that could instead be directed to advance student learning. Disrupting traditional and ineffective practices of music teacher PD using these strategies has wide-ranging and long-term implications for positive change in the field of music education.

References

Bauer W. I. (2007). Research on professional development for experienced music teachers. *Journal of Music Teacher Education*, *17*(1), 12–21. https://doi.org/10.1177/10570837070170010105

Bautista, A., & Ortega-Ruíz, R. (2015). Teacher professional development: International perspectives and approaches. *Psychology, Society, and Education*, *7*(3), 240–251. https://doi.org/10.25115/psye.v7i3.1020

Bautista, A., Toh, G. Z., & Wong, J. (2018). Primary school music teachers' professional development motivations, needs, and preferences: Does specialization make a difference? *Musicae Scientiae*, *22*(2), 196–223. https://doi.org/10.1177/1029864916678654

Bautista, A., Yau, X., & Wong, J. (2017). High-quality music teacher professional development: A review of the literature. *Music Education Research*, *19*(4), 455–469. https://doi.org/10.1080/14613808.2016.1249357

Blackley, S., & Sheffield, R. (2015). Digital andragogy: A richer blend of initial teacher education in the 21st century. *Issues in Educational Research*, *25*(4), 397–414.

Bowles, C. (2002). The self-expressed professional development needs of music educators. *Update: Applications of Research in Music Education*, *21*(2), 35–41. https://doi.org/10.1177/87551233020210020701

Buchanan, R., Scott, J. A., Pease-Alvarez, L., & Clark, M. (2022). Common ground is not enough: The situated and dynamic process of collaboration in a multiagency teacher professional development project. *Teaching and Teacher Education, 117*, 103764. https://doi.org/10.1016/j.tate.2022.103764

Bush, J. E. (2007). Importance of various professional development opportunities and workshop topics as determined by in-service music teachers. *Journal of Music Teacher Education, 16*(2), 10–18. https://doi.org/10.1177/10570837070160020103

Campbell, M. R. (2014). Inquiry and synthesis in pre-service music teacher education. In M. Kaschub, & J. Smith (Eds.), *Promising practices in 21st century music teacher education* (pp. 149–173). Oxford University Press.

Campbell, M. R., & Barrett, J. R. (2013). Music teacher education and continuous professional development. *School Music News, 77*, 17–22.

Conway, C. M. (2001). What has research told us about the beginning music teacher? *Journal of Music Teacher Education, 10*(2), 14–22. https://doi.org/10.1177/10570837010100020104

Conway, C. M., & Edgar, S. N. (2014). Inservice Music Teacher Professional Development. In C. M. Conway (Ed.), *The Oxford handbook of qualitative research in American music education* (pp. 479–500). Oxford University Press. https://doi.org/10.1093/oxfordhb/9780199844272.013.025

Craig, C. J. (2009). Research in the midst of organized school reform: Versions of teacher community in tension. *American Educational Research Journal, 46*(2), 598–619. https://doi.org/10.3102/0002831208330213.

Danielson, C. (2013). *Enhancing professional practice: A framework for teaching* (2nd ed.). Association for Supervision and Curriculum Development.

Darling-Hammond, L. (1990). Instructional policy into practice: "The power of the bottom over the top." *Educational Evaluation and Policy Analysis, 12*(3), 339–347. https://doi.org/10.2307/1164357

Darling-Hammond, L. (2010). Teaching for deeper learning: Developing a thinking pedagogy. In A. P. C. Avila, C. Hui, J. H. Lin, J. C. Peng Tam, & J. C. Lim (Eds.), *Rethinking educational paradigms: Moving from good to great. CJ Koh Professorial Lecture Series No. 5* (pp. 13–18). Office of Education Research, National Institute of Education.

Darling-Hammond, L., Bastian, K. C., Berry, B., Carver-Thomas, D., Kini, T., Levin, S., & McDiarmid, G. W. (2022). Educator supply, demand, and quality in North Carolina: Current status and recommendations. Research Brief. *Learning Policy Institute*. https://eric.ed.gov/?id=ED617602

Darling-Hammond, L., Chung Wei, R., Andree, A., Richardson, N., & Orphanos, S. (2009). *Professional learning in the learning profession: A status report on teacher development in the United States and abroad.* National Staff Development Council, Stanford University.

Darling-Hammond, L., & McLaughlin, M. W. (1995). Policies that support professional development in an era of reform. *Phi Delta Kappan, 76*(8), 597–604. https://doi.org/10.1177/003172171109200622

Desimone, L. M. (2009). Improving impact studies of teachers' professional development: Toward better conceptualizations and measures. *Educational Researcher, 38*(3), 181–199. https://doi.org/10.3102/0013189X08331140

Desimone, L. M. (2011). A primer on effective professional development. *Phi Delta Kappan, 92*(6), 68–71. https://doi.org/10.1177/003172171109200616

Desimone, L. M., & Garet, M. S. (2015). Best practices in teacher's professional development in the United States. *Psychology, Society & Education, 7*, 252–263.

Desimone, L., Smith, T. M., & Phillips, K. (2013). Linking student achievement growth to professional development participation and changes in instruction: A longitudinal study of elementary students and teachers in title I schools. *Teachers College Record, 115*(5), 1–46

Draves, T. J. (2017). Instrumental music educators' experiences in a professional development course. *Update: Applications of Research in Music Education, 35*(3), 38–45. https://doi.org/10.1177/8755123316634174

Eros, J. (2011). The career cycle and the second stage of teaching: Implications for policy and professional development. *Arts Education Policy Review, 112*(2), 65–70. https://doi.org/10.1080/10632913.2011.546683

Eros, J. (2013). Second-stage music teachers' perceptions of their professional development. *Journal of Music Teacher Education, 22*(2), 20–33. https://doi.org/10.1177/1057083712438771

Fermanich, M. L. (2011). Money for music education: A district analysis of the how, what, and where of spending for music education. *Journal of Education Finance 37*(2), 130–149. www.muse.jhu.edu/article/456335

Good, T. L., & Lavigne, A. L. (2017). *Looking in classrooms*. Routledge.

Gruenewald, D. A. (2003). The best of both worlds: A critical pedagogy of place. *Educational Researcher, 32*(4) 3–12. https://doi.org/10.3102/0013189X032004003

Hammel, A. M. (2007). Professional development research in general education. *Journal of Music Teacher Education, 17*(1), 22–32. https://doi.org/10.1177/10570837070170010106

Hartz, B., Derges-Kastner, J., Robbins, J., & Stanley, A. M. (2014, April 10–12). *Renewed, reinvigorated, recharged: The voices of experienced teachers on their self-initiated professional development.* Paper presented at the National Association for Music Education Music Research and Teacher Education Conference, St. Louis, MO.

Hattie, J. (2009). *Visible learning: A synthesis of over 800 meta-analyses relating to achievement.* Routledge.

Haug, B. S., & Mork, S. M. (2021). Taking 21st century skills from vision to classroom: What teachers highlight as supportive professional development in the light of new demands from educational reforms. *Teaching and Teacher Education, 100,* 103286. https://doi.org/10.1016/j.tate.2021.103286

Hill, H. C. (2009). Fixing teacher professional development. *Phi Delta Kappan, 90*(7), 470–476. https://doi.org/10.1177/003172170909000705

Horn, M. B., & Goldstein, M. (2018). Putting school budgets in teachers' hands: What if end-users in the classroom made purchasing decisions? *Education Next, 18*(4), 82–83.

Johnson, D. C., & Howell, G. (2009, September 10–12). *Drop-out prevention among at-risk students through integrated arts education: A school-university-community partnership* [Poster presentation]. Society for Music Teacher Education Symposium. Greensboro, NC.

Johnson, D. C., & Stanley, A. M. (2021). Exploring rural music teachers' perceptions and practices via an online professional development course. *Journal of Music Teacher Education, 3*(30), 99–114. https://doi.org/10.1177/10570837211008658

Johnson, D. C., Stanley, A. M., & Nowak, T. (2021, September 23–25). *Exploring the rural music teacher experience through online professional development.* Research Presentation at the Society for Music Teacher Education Symposium.

Johnson, D. C., Stanley, A. M., Falter, H. E., Greene, J. L. R., Moore, H. L., Paparone, S., Smith, J. C., & Snell, A. H. (2019). Reflections on music teacher professional development: Teacher-generated policies and practices. *Arts Education Policy Review, 120*(4), 208–200. https://doi.org/10.1080/10632913.2018.1468839

Kane, T. J., & Staiger, D. O. (2008). Estimating teacher impacts on student achievement: An experimental evaluation. *National Bureau of Economic Research*, Cambridge, MA. https://doi:10.3386/w14607

Kennedy, M. M. (2016). How does professional development improve teaching? *Review of Educational Research, 86*, 945–980. https://doi:10.3102/0034654315626800

Koner, K., & Eros, J. (2019). Professional development for the experienced music educator: A review of recent literature. *Update: Applications of Research in Music Education, 37*(3), 12–19. https://doi.org/10.1177/8755123318812426

Korthagen, F. A., Kim, Y. M., & Greene, W. L. (2012). *Teaching and learning from within: A core reflection approach to quality and inspiration in education.* Routledge.

Lai, M. K., & McNaughton, S. (2016). The impact of data use professional development on student achievement. *Teaching and Teacher Education, 60*, 434–44 https://doi.org/10.1016/j.tate.2016.07.005

Meissel, K., Parr, J. M., & Timperley, H. S. (2016). Can professional development of teachers reduce disparity in student achievement? *Teaching and Teacher Education*, *58*, 163–173. https://doi.org/10.1016/j.tate.2016.05.013

Millican, J. S. (2008). A new framework for music education knowledge and skill. *Journal of Music Teacher Education*, *18*(1), 67–78. https://doi.org/10.1177/1057083708323146

National Association for Music Education. (2015a). *Professional Development eKit*. https://nafme.org/my-classroom/professional-development/professional-development-ekit

National Association for Music Education. (2015b). *Strategic Plan (2016–2021)*. https://nafme.org/wp-content/uploads/2014/06/Strategic-Plan_revised-2016.pdf

Noblit, G., Corbett, D., & Wilson, B. (2000). *The arts and education reform: Lesson from a four-year evaluation of the A+ Schools program, 1995–1999*. The Thomas S. Kenan Institute for the Arts.

Noblit, G., Corbett, D., Wilson, B., & McKinney, M. (2009). *Creating and sustaining arts-based school reform: The A+ Schools Program*. Routledge.

Odden, A., Archibald, S., Fermanich, M., & Gallagher, H. A. (2002). A cost framework for professional development. *Journal of Education Finance* *28*(1), 51–74.

Reynolds, A., Robbins, J., Bauer, W., Stanley, A. M., & Eros, J. (2010, March 25-27). *Professional development for experienced music teachers: Learning in community*. Paper presented at the Music Teachers National Conference, Anaheim, CA.

Rickels, D. A., & Brewer, W. D. (2017). Facebook band director's group: Member usage behaviors and perceived satisfaction for meeting professional development needs. *Journal of Music Teacher Education*, *26*(3), 77–92. https://doi.org/10.1177/1057083717692380

Rolandson, D. M., & Ross-Hekkel, L. E. (2022). Virtual professional learning communities: A case study in rural music teacher professional development. *Journal of Music Teacher Education*, *31*(3), 81–94. https://doi.org/10.1177/10570837221077430

Schmidt, P., & Robbins, J. (2011). Looking backwards to reach forward: A strategic architecture for professional development in music education. *Arts Education Policy Review*, *112*(2), 95–103.

Schwab, J. J. (1959/1978). The "impossible" role of the teacher in progressive education. In I. Westbury & N. Wilkof (Eds.), *Science, curriculum and liberal education: Selected essays* (pp. 167–183). University of Chicago Press.

Simonsen, B., Freeman, J., Myers, D., Dooley, K., Maddock, E., Kern, L., & Byun, S. (2020). The effects of targeted professional development on teachers' use of empirically supported classroom management practices. *Journal of Positive Behavior Interventions*, *22*(1), 3–14. https://doi.org/10.1177/1098300719859615

Stanley, A. M., Snell, A., & Edgar, S. (2014). Collaboration as effective music professional development: Success stories from the field. *Journal of Music Teacher Education, 24*(1), 76–88. https://doi.org/10.1177/1057083713502731

Tobias, E. (2014). 21st century musicianship through digital media and participatory culture. Inquiry and synthesis in pre-service music teacher education. In M. Kaschub & J. Smith (Eds.), *Promising practices in 21st century music teacher education* (pp. 205–230). Oxford University Press.

Tucker, O. G. (2020). Supporting the development of agency in music teacher education. *Journal of Music Teacher Education, 29*(3), 24–36.

Upitis, R., & Brook, J. (2017). How much professional development is enough? Meeting the needs of independent music teachers learning to use a digital tool. *International Journal of Music Education, 35*(1), 93–106. https://doi.org/10.1177/0255761415619426

Wesolowski, B. C., Alsop, M. A., Athanas, M. I., & Dean, L. H. (2021). On the quality of professional development in the United States: Examining music educators' experiences, sentiments, and emotions. *International Journal of Music Education*, 02557614211019149. https://doi.org/10.1177/02557614211019149

West, J. J., Stanley, A. M., & Appova, A. K. (2022). Exogenous shocks and teachers' motivation to earn: Pandemic and professional development in the United States. *International Journal for Research in Education, 46*(2), 261–308. http://doi.org/10.36771/ijre.46.2.22-pp261-308

West, J. J., Stanley, A. M., Bowers, J. P., & Isbell, D. S. (2021). Attrition,(de) motivation, and "effective" music teacher professional development: An instrumental case study. *Bulletin of the Council for Research in Music Education*, (229), 7–28. https://doi.org/10.5406/bulcouresmusedu.229.0007

Index

Note: Figures are indicated by *italics*.

www.ingramcontent.com/pod-product-compliance
Lightning Source LLC
LaVergne TN
LVHW010933110826
845149LV00013B/2572